"A dear friend of mine in France seriousl[ ]
reading Gilles Deleuze. He did return t[ ]
have done so sooner had he been able to [ ] ....o excellent
volume. The author carefully and masterfully introduces us to
Deleuze. One of the philosopher's great appeals is his creative
alternatives to typical atheism. Some of it *sounds* Christian: his
celebration of difference; his critique of the chain of being; his
appeal to dynamic, rather than static, ways of living. But it all ends
up a brilliant caricature, and Watkin helps us see where Deleuze
misses the boat. To boot, his presentation of the Christian worldview is marvelous. Why should any of this matter? If you think
you have not been influenced by French poststructuralism, you
need to think again. It's in the cultural air we breathe. Watkin
helps us clear away the smog. As someone I sat next to during a
rather technical speech told me: 'I don't understand a lot of this,
but I'm glad the speaker is on our side!' Watkin does understand
it, and he is on our side."
    —**William Edgar**, Professor of Apologetics, Westminster
        Theological Seminary

"Cutting through the often-impenetrable language of French
poststructuralism, Chris Watkin has done us all a service.
Few philosophers of the past fifty years have carried forward
Nietzsche's 'inverted Platonism' (i.e., nihilism) more compel-
lingly than Deleuze. Besides letting Deleuze's own views come
through clearly, Watkin supplies an astute critique and hopeful
alternative in Christian eschatology."
    —**Michael Horton**, J. Gresham Machen Professor of
        Systematic Theology and Apologetics, Westminster
        Seminary California

"Watkin affords the Christian believer another fine entrée to participate in the philosophical life to which all humans are born:

to understand both how Gilles Deleuze profoundly voiced our time, and also how very cool (adding to Peter Leithart's designation of 'weird'!) is the philosophizing that Christianity engenders. Christianity's welcoming approach of the gospel breaks in and breaks open human thought and culture, as David Kettle describes it, winsomely rendering it more itself than it could otherwise be. And that's true of Deleuze just as it was of Plato."

—**Esther Lightcap Meek**, Professor of Philosophy, Geneva College; author, *Loving to Know: Introducing Covenant Epistemology*

"As with his previous books on Derrida and Foucault, Christopher Watkin once more demonstrates what an immense blessing he is to the Christian community as he holds our hands and guides us expertly through the complex world of Gilles Deleuze—a world that has shaped, and continues to shape in profound ways, our contemporary Western society. It is the model of Watkin's engagement that is so important, and at times so discomforting. He will not let us get away with superficial and simplistic descriptions, analyses, and critiques. Rather, he demonstrates the Christian virtue of careful and sympathetic listening so necessary in the process of cultural apologetics and biblical refutation. Finally, as with his other works in this series, one finishes Watkin's analysis with wonderment, praising God for the depth, the breadth, and the radical nature of the Christian worldview and the person and work of Jesus Christ."

—**Dan Strange**, Director, Oak Hill College, London

"The hurricane that was postmodernity may have blown itself out, yet many left to deal with the wreckage still want to know what happened. What, after the 'death' of God in the 1960s, was still holding up the edifice of traditional Western philosophy that required further dismantling? One of the best answers I've come across yet is in Christopher Watkin's little gem of a book, on the most important twentieth-century French philosopher you've never heard of: Gilles Deleuze. This deep dive into the concept of *difference* explains why postmodern philosophy is less a footnote to Plato than a crushing of his heel. Getting a better grasp on Deleuze even yields insights into the forces shaping the outlooks and experience of those who belong to Gen X, Y, or Z. Not only that: Watkin's book comes with a bonus, namely, a comparison and contrast of Deleuze's way of thinking with that of the Bible. This is must reading for thinking Christians."

—**Kevin J. Vanhoozer**, Research Professor of Systematic Theology, Trinity Evangelical Divinity School

Gilles
DELEUZE

GREAT THINKERS

A Series

Series Editor
Nathan D. Shannon

AVAILABLE IN THE GREAT THINKERS SERIES

Thomas Aquinas, by K. Scott Oliphint
Francis Bacon, by David C. Innes
Richard Dawkins, by Ransom H. Poythress
Gilles Deleuze, by Christopher Watkin
Jacques Derrida, by Christopher Watkin
Michel Foucault, by Christopher Watkin
G. W. F. Hegel, by Shao Kai Tseng
David Hume, by James N. Anderson
Immanuel Kant, by Shao Kai Tseng
Karl Marx, by William D. Dennison
Karl Rahner, by Camden M. Bucey

FORTHCOMING

Karl Barth, by Shao Kai Tseng
Friedrich Nietzsche, by Carl R. Trueman
Alvin Plantinga, by Greg Welty
Plato, by David Talcott
Adam Smith, by Jan van Vliet

Gilles
DELEUZE

Christopher Watkin

P&R PUBLISHING
P.O. BOX 817 • PHILLIPSBURG • NEW JERSEY 08865-0817

Scripture quotations are from The ESV® Bible (The Holy Bible, English Standard Version®), copyright © 2001 by Crossway, a publishing ministry of Good News Publishers. Used by permission. All rights reserved.

Italics within Scripture quotations indicate emphasis added.

ISBN: 978-1-62995-743-2 (pbk)
ISBN: 978-1-62995-744-9 (ePub)
ISBN: 978-1-62995-745-6 (Mobi)

Printed in the United States of America

Library of Congress Cataloging-in-Publication Data

Names: Watkin, Christopher, author.
Title: Gilles Deleuze / Christopher Watkin.
Description: Phillipsburg, New Jersey : P&R Publishing, 2020. | Series:
  Great thinkers | Includes bibliographical references and index. |
  Summary: "Gilles Deleuze's ideas are indispensable to understanding how
  truth and ethics no longer have theological reference points. Watkin's
  biblical critique enables us to culturally reengage with our
  Deleuze-influenced society"-- Provided by publisher.
Identifiers: LCCN 2020001429 | ISBN 9781629957432 (paperback) | ISBN
  9781629957449 (epub) | ISBN 9781629957456 (mobi)
Subjects: LCSH: Deleuze, Gilles, 1925-1995.
Classification: LCC B2430.D454 W38 2020 | DDC 194--dc23
LC record available at https://lccn.loc.gov/2020001429

For little Emma

CONTENTS

SERIES INTRODUCTION

Amid the rise and fall of nations and civilizations, the influence of a few great minds has been profound. Some of these remain relatively obscure even as their thought shapes our world; others have become household names. As we engage our cultural and social contexts as ambassadors and witnesses for Christ, we must identify and test against the Word those thinkers who have so singularly formed the present age.

The Great Thinkers series is designed to meet the need for critically assessing the seminal thoughts of these thinkers. Great Thinkers hosts a colorful roster of authors analyzing primary source material against a background of historical contextual issues, and providing rich theological assessment and response from a Reformed perspective.

Each author was invited to meet a threefold goal, so that each Great Thinkers volume is, first, *academically informed*. The brevity of Great Thinkers volumes sets a premium on each author's command of the subject matter and on the secondary discussions that have shaped each thinker's influence. Our authors identify the most influential features of their thinkers' work and address them with precision and insight. Second, the series maintains a high standard of *biblical and theological faithfulness*. Each volume stands on an epistemic commitment to "the whole counsel of God" (Acts 20:27), and is thereby equipped for fruitful critical engagement. Finally, Great Thinkers texts are *accessible*, not burdened with jargon or unnecessarily difficult vocabulary. The goal is to inform and equip the reader as effectively as possible through clear writing, relevant analysis, and incisive, constructive critique. My hope is that this series will distinguish itself by striking with biblical faithfulness and the riches of the Reformed tradition at the central nerves of culture, cultural history, and intellectual heritage.

Bryce Craig, president of P&R Publishing, deserves hearty thanks for his initiative and encouragement in setting the series in motion and seeing it through. Many thanks as well to P&R's director of academic development, John Hughes, who has assumed, with cool efficiency, nearly every role on the production side of each volume. The Rev. Mark Moser carried much of the burden in the initial design of the series, acquisitions, and editing of the first several volumes. And the expert participation of Amanda Martin, P&R's editorial director, was essential at every turn. I have long admired P&R Publishing's commitment, steadfast now for over eighty-five years, to publishing excellent books promoting biblical understanding and cultural awareness, especially in the area of Christian apologetics. Sincere thanks to P&R, to these fine brothers and sisters, and to several others not mentioned here for the opportunity to serve as editor of the Great Thinkers series.

Nathan D. Shannon
Seoul, Korea

FOREWORD

Christians are likely to recoil at the philosophy of Gilles Deleuze (1925–95), the subject of this book. He seems to be hostile to everything Christians love and to approve what Christians hate.

For Deleuze, the bogeyman of the history of philosophy is the concept of transcendence, the belief in two worlds—heaven and earth, this world and the next. Good Nietzschean that he is, Deleuze views transcendence as an enemy to life, requiring self-renunciation, demanding restraint of "lower" bodily desires, seducing humans to seek fulfillment elsewhere, grinding the masses down to mousy conformity. Platonism and Christianity are variant forms of the ontology and politics of transcendence, and both are targets of Deleuze's effort to confine philosophy to a plane of immanence. He aims to flatten the transcendent, hierarchical intellectual "tree" into a complex, nonhierarchical "stem system," to replace the arboreal with the rhizomic.

Philosophy, Deleuze says, is always political. Philosophers work back to front, not from observation and reflection on the way things are to ethical and political conclusions, but from a desired polity down to an ontology to justify it. First imagine utopia; then rough in its foundations. Transcendence invents static essences to fix the differences that teem across the plane of immanence. Plato's dogmatic image of thought preserves political order and stability by turning philosophy itself into a "policing action" that judges between true and false. Deleuze advocates an ontology of liberation to break the chains and permit an infinite proliferation of styles of life.

Here is a philosopher who dashes off casual blasphemies such as "God is a lobster," who longs to dismantle the male/female binary to make room for a "thousand tiny sexes," who dissolves God even though (or because) the dissolution of the "self" necessarily follows, who blurs the relationship between humanity and the world, who wishes, once and for all, to erase from philosophy the last faint trace of theology.

Christians are likely to recoil, *and* to retreat, perhaps to the haven of a semi-Platonized Christianity, an unreflective realism, a worldview that gives priority to the static, the timeless, the safe. In this astonishingly patient and lucid introduction, Christopher Watkin neither recoils nor retreats. He does not play safe but dares to pay sympathetic attention. *Audi alteram partem*—"listen to the other part"—is his motto and method.

It pays off. By comparing Deleuze with the Bible, Watkin shows that Christian truth is far weirder than we realize. At times, the weirdness flames out when Deleuze unknowingly brushes up against biblical truth. To overturn Plato, Deleuze insists that there's no identity beyond or beneath difference and denies the primacy of the original over the copy, the priority of the model to the image. He thinks the same critique applies to Christianity, but he is late to the party. Following out the logic of the New Testament, Trinitarian theologians of the fourth century had already overturned Plato in just these ways. Within the Trinity there is no undifferentiated One above or beneath the Three, and within the Trinity the "image of the invisible God" is coeternal, even consubstantial, with the

Father whom he images. In the triune God, image and copy are as transcendent and primordial as the original and model.

At other times, Deleuzean insights call attention to underdeveloped possibilities of biblical thought. Essence, he says, is not being, but the power to become, a definition that may dovetail with the Bible's eschatological ontology: "what we will be has not yet appeared" (1 John 3:2). Borrowing from Henri Bergson, Deleuze recognizes that our perceptions in the present are indwelt by memories of past experience. We perceive a mug *as* a mug only because we have encountered other mugs and know their form and purpose. This mutual enfoldment of times might be taken as a vestige of the perichoretic relations of the persons of the Trinity.

Scripture "diagonalizes" Plato and Deleuze, cutting across radical critique and dogmatic transcendence to expose their hidden agreement. Deleuze turns Plato on his head without shattering the Platonic apparatus itself. Plato's ideas cannot become incarnate, nor does Deleuze's virtual, the transcendental condition of possibility of the actual. For both, the key to reality never makes itself known as sensible, visible, tangible. Scripture has more explosive strength. As John proclaims, the Word that is from the beginning, the Word in whom all things cohere, the Word that is the condition of possibility for all that is—*that* Word of life has been seen, touched, handled, heard. The Bible is more radical than Deleuze, its teaching on creation and incarnation *more* affirmative of immanence, particularity, matter, time, and even difference.

Watkin's volume is more than an introduction to Deleuze, more even than a model of bold Christian engagement with modern atheism. It is a remarkable piece of Christian philosophy in its own right, and will edify even those whose instinct is to recoil and retreat.

Peter J. Leithart
Beth-Elim
Gardendale, Alabama

ACKNOWLEDGMENTS

I am particularly grateful to Sean Bowden for commenting on a draft of Part 1 and providing valuable feedback on my reading of Deleuze, and to Daniel Strange, Charlie Butler, Graham Shearer, and Timothy Keller for providing encouragement for my writing when I might otherwise have laid down my pen. This is the third of my contributions to the P&R Great Thinkers series, discussing three giants who have helped shape much in our culture over the past half-century and more: Jacques Derrida, Michel Foucault, and Gilles Deleuze. I am grateful to series editor Nathan Shannon and P&R Director of Academic Development John Hughes for encouraging my vision to complete this trilogy of studies. The exercise has immeasurably enriched my own understanding of how Reformed theology and modern and contemporary thought can be brought into constructive conversation, and I hope and pray that something in these books might provide a similar service to others. Convention and enthusiasm join forces in directing me to extend my deepest, heartfelt thanks to my wife, Alison, whose sharpness of mind and tireless love are a source not only of many of the thoughts in these pages but also of the strength and vision without which they would never have been written down at all. More than patience, more than inspiration, you have provided, once again, this book's sine qua non. *Soli deo gloria.*

ABBREVIATIONS

AO	*Anti-Oedipus*
ATP	*A Thousand Plateaus*
B	*Bergsonism*
C2	*Cinema 2: The Time-Image*
D	*Dialogues*
DI	*Desert Islands*
DR	*Difference and Repetition*
ECC	*Essays Critical and Clinical*
EPS	*Expressionism in Philosophy: Spinoza*
ES	*Empiricism and Subjectivity*
F	*Foucault*
FBLS	*Francis Bacon: The Logic of Sensation*
FLB	*The Fold: Leibniz and the Baroque*
LS	*The Logic of Sense*
NaP	*Nietzsche and Philosophy*
Ne	*Negotiations, 1972–1990*
PI	*Pure Immanence*
PS	*Proust and Signs*
SPP	*Spinoza: Practical Philosophy*

2RM   *Two Regimes of Madness: Texts and Interviews 1975–1995*

WIP   *What Is Philosophy?*

INTRODUCTION

One of the ugly and besetting sins of academics is our tendency to complain about our students. They are lazy; they are intellectually incurious; they seek to cut corners and do the least work possible; they will complete no work unless they are awarded a mark for it; and so on. When we peel back the layers of this self-righteous litany, however, it often amounts to little more than saying, "My students are not like me"—or, more accurately, "My jaundiced view of my students is not like the sparkling image I have of myself." This, if we stop to think about it, is probably a very good thing both for ourselves and for our students.

Once in a while, however, a colleague will offer a judgment of a student that, far from being high-handedly dismissive, perfectly captures something that you always knew but couldn't put words to. I vividly remember hearing one such incisive comment, in the course of a telephone conversation in which a colleague was inviting me to examine a doctoral candidate in contemporary French thought. At one point in the conversation, she threw in a remark to the effect that "the candidate is good, but she's a member of the church of Deleuze." It wasn't a condemnation—more an observation. For this candidate, it was Gilles Deleuze or bust: her intellectual Bible was Deleuze-only; she was an orthodox Deleuzian and did not suffer heretics gladly.

Deleuze can do that to you. He is one of those French thinkers—Foucault is another, Derrida perhaps a little less so—who continue to gather passionate disciples ready to dedicate the best years of their intellectual lives to becoming more Deleuzian than thou. This is no more meant as a condemnation than was my colleague's comment on the phone. Deleuze, as we will see, offers a comprehensive and in many ways a compelling account of reality, humanity, and politics that has fascinated and continues to fascinate many. But that is not why I have written this book on him for a Christian publisher. Deleuze is less cited than Foucault and often as difficult to read as Derrida, so why should Christians in particular and curious readers in general bother to expend their precious energy on understanding and engaging with his thought? Let me offer four reasons up front.

My first reason to read Deleuze is not the most exciting of the bunch, but it serves as a foundation for the following three: Deleuze is indispensable if we want to come to terms with the period in mid- to late-twentieth-century thinking that has—for better or, mostly, for worse—often carried the label *postmodern*.[1] In my own institution as well as in many others, a steady stream of PhD theses engage with Deleuze's thought. The journal *Deleuze Studies*, published by Edinburgh University Press, now runs to twelve volumes, and the book series Plateaus—New Directions in Deleuze Studies (also with EUP) boasts over thirty

---

1. The term *postmodern* appears in Deleuze's works very infrequently. It occurs in brief references to Jean-François Lyotard's *The Postmodern Condition*, and in a critical reading of Frederic Jameson's distinction between "modernism" and "postmodernism" (*F*, xxiii–xxv). Deleuze and Guattari were, as Philip Goodchild rightly notes, "scornful of the notion of 'postmodernity,'" in *Deleuze and Guattari: An Introduction to the Politics of Desire* (London: Sage, 1996), 2.

titles. For what it's worth, at the time of writing, Google Books records 1.1 million references to Deleuze.

If Deleuze rivals Foucault in the volume of academic activity that his writing generates these days, he rivals Derrida in its breadth. He has made defining contributions well beyond philosophy to disciplines as diverse as psychoanalysis, feminism, cinema, literature, ecology, queer theory, and politics, and this is reflected in the breadth of books on his thought. The list of titles beginning *Deleuze and . . .* runs to eighty volumes, including *Deleuze and Education*, *Deleuze and Sex*, *Deleuze and Art*, *Deleuze and Race*, and not forgetting *Deleuze and Theology* and *Deleuze and Religion*.

Deleuze's writing is not of purely academic interest, however, and this brings me to my second reason why Christians would do well to understand and engage with his thought. The extent to which Deleuze has both predicted and helped shape contemporary Western society is rivaled among recent French thinkers only perhaps by Foucault, and it was Foucault himself who famously predicted in 1970 that "perhaps one day, this century will be known as Deleuzian" (*"Un jour peut-être, le siècle sera Deleuzien"*).[2] If Derrida and Foucault help us to understand how our society got where it is today, then perhaps Deleuze best of all can help us to understand where it may be headed tomorrow.

Moving now to the substance of Deleuze's thought, my third reason to commend him to your readerly attention is that he questions the self-evident with an uncanny and unusual tenacity. He takes some of the most prized shibboleths of our contemporary society, such as the truism that "we are all human deep down" and the value of multiculturalism, and reveals in them

---

2. Michel Foucault, "Theatrum Philosophicum," in *Aesthetics, Method, and Epistemology*, ed. James D. Faubion, trans. R. Hurley et al., *Essential Works of Foucault 1954–84*, 2 (New York: New Press, 1998), 343. For a discussion of the complex and ambiguous meanings of the remark, see *Aesthetics, Method and Epistemology*, xxi–xxii.

surprising and dangerous currents of oppression.[3] We may or may not agree with his analysis, but it certainly fulfills one of the characteristics of all good philosophy: it makes us think again about things we thought we knew, and it invites us to see things differently.

Spread throughout Deleuze's work, from the 1968/1994 *Difference and Repetition* to the 1993/1998 *Essays Critical and Clinical*, are references to the so-called "underground man" in Fyodor Dostoyevsky's *Notes from the Underground*. What intrigues Deleuze about Dostoyevsky's nameless antihero is his refusal to fall into line with accepted commonplaces. He "cannot keep two and two from making four" but "will not RESIGN himself to it either (*he prefers that two and two not make four*)" (*ECC*, 81–82, emphasis original). The underground man exemplifies the trait that, according to Deleuze, Dostoyevsky shares with other great novelists, namely, that "things remain enigmatic yet nonarbitrary," yielding "a new logic, definitely a logic, but one that grasps the innermost depths of life and death without leading us back to reason" (*ECC*, 82).

Always to question the self-evident soon becomes tiresome and predictable, but never to do so can quickly reveal itself to be naive and dangerous. What Deleuze commends in Dostoyevsky's underground man is finding the right level of questioning, the level that reveals the enigmatic nature of our commonsense assumptions without shrugging them off as completely arbitrary. This idea of finding the "enigmatic yet nonarbitrary" sweet spot of questioning also serves as a good first introduction to

---

3. This move of revealing society's sacred cows to be cruel and oppressive resembles Michel Foucault's unmasking of the supposed humanitarianism of the care of those with mental illness in the nineteenth century, and the "disciplinary power" that characterizes modern penitentiary systems that no longer practice torture or execution. See my *Michel Foucault*, Great Thinkers (Phillipsburg, NJ: P&R Publishing, 2018).

Deleuze's own approach to problems in philosophy and society. The common caricature of postmodernism is that it holds meanings and values to be, precisely, arbitrary. Let it be said very clearly at the outset of this book that Deleuze unambiguously rejects this view. But the no less common reaction to this idea that meanings and values are arbitrary for postmodernism is that meanings and values are matters of common sense, a position that Deleuze rejects just as emphatically. He is neither a postmodernist nor an enemy of postmodernism here; his thought inhabits an enigmatic region that can be reduced neither to arbitrariness nor to merely regurgitating what "everyone knows."

Many philosophers have a tendency to begin by assuming that we all already agree on the rules of analysis and logic, and then proceed to squabble over who is applying those rules most consistently or most effectively. Rather than denouncing those who are not acting according to the accepted laws of the game, as we will see below, Deleuze raises the question whether we are playing by the right rules to begin with.[4] Who cares who scores the most touchdowns if the game that we are supposed to be playing is baseball? Whether we end up agreeing with Deleuze or not, one effect of this questioning of commonplace assumptions is that he shows us that we all think and see the world and ourselves in a particular way, and that we could very well see them in a different way. Furthermore, if we accept—as surely we must—that new ways of seeing the world make possible new ways of being and acting in it, then we begin to see some of the transformative potential of Deleuzian thought. Deleuze wants to make us see the world differently, in order that we may act differently in it.

The fourth and final reason I will offer for engaging with

4. This point is made by Claire Colebrook, *Understanding Deleuze* (Sydney: Allen and Unwin, 2003), 4.

Deleuze's thought is perhaps of special interest to Christian readers: Deleuze challenges common Christian and new atheistic attitudes to the consequences of the death of God. Two equally egregious misunderstandings haunt the reception of the death of God. On the one hand, Christians are often far too hasty to say that, without God, all we are left with is the absence of all truth, moral anarchy, and meaninglessness.[5] On the other hand, a view common among the new atheists asserts that when we take God out of the picture, pretty much everything else can stay just as it was, including our understanding of existence, truth, meaning, and ethics.[6] There is, to be sure, a grain of truth in both these positions. The new atheists are correct that when we attempt to think without God, we do not necessarily have to abandon notions of truth or ethics altogether. The hasty Christians are correct that when we attempt to think without God, we cannot persist with the very same notions of truth and ethics that prevailed when God was in the picture. But both positions move too quickly, and go too far, in prosecuting their respective arguments.

What Deleuze gives us, against the background of this simplifying dichotomy, is a very sophisticated account of what happens to truth and ethics in a system of thought that does not rely on God as traditionally understood, a system that will necessarily be radically different from one that does rely on God. Of course it will: to paraphrase Deleuze in the words of a now-classic meme, "one does not simply" take God out of the picture. Getting rid of

5. The logic of this sort of position is that if there is no moral law such as the Bible offers—transcendent, underwritten by God, absolute, and universal—then there can be no morality at all. It is telling that Nietzsche is frequently framed as the poster boy for this moral vacuum, whereas Deleuze takes from Nietzsche an ethics that, while it is very far from the Christian position and not without its own problems, is not an ethical nihilism.

6. I discuss some of the problems with this position under the banner of *imitative atheism* in *Difficult Atheism: Post-Theological Thinking in Alain Badiou, Jean-Luc Nancy and Quentin Meillassoux* (Edinburgh: Edinburgh University Press, 2011).

God changes everything, including what we mean by existence, truth, and ethics, and Christian critics of nonreligious thought would do well to move beyond the mantra of "no God = no truth = no ethics."

Deleuze in Historical and Intellectual Context

To situate Deleuze in his historical and intellectual context, as Claire Colebrook rightly notes, is a spectacularly un-Deleuzian thing to do because it goes against Deleuze's own way of challenging the idea of a neatly unfolding succession of intellectual influences and oppositions.[7] Nevertheless, we may begin to understand Deleuze's thought—as does Colebrook herself—in the context of two important mid-twentieth-century intellectual currents. The first of these is structuralism, according to which we experience the world only through the structures of representation that our thought and language have imposed on it, much in the same way as the meaning of the pieces on a chessboard is given by the overall structure and rules of the game: it is the rules and the board that make a bishop a "bishop" and a knight a "knight," not the individual plastic or metal objects sitting on the board. If I lose one of my "bishops," I can substitute any old object of the right size, and the game can continue unhampered.

Deleuze, as we will see, rejects as hopelessly anthropocentric the structuralist position that human language and human structures give the world its meaning. Whereas structuralism reserves a privileged place for human language in imposing differences and distinctions on a fundamentally undifferentiated reality, Deleuze understands the world to be already proliferating with differences, and human language in fact reduces difference rather

---

7. Claire Colebrook, *Gilles Deleuze*, Routledge Critical Thinkers (London: Routledge, 2001), 8.

than creates it. Furthermore, for Deleuze, human language offers only one system of differences among many others, including genetic, chromatic, and chemical.[8]

The second intellectual current from which Deleuze's thought distances itself is phenomenology, with its principle that all knowledge begins with phenomena, with how things appear to me, regardless of what those things may or not be in themselves. As with structuralism, this position betrays for Deleuze an unwarranted anthropocentric bias: why should the first-person perception of the human subject be the privileged locus of all meaning? For Deleuze, human meanings and structures are merely one small part of a much larger picture, and neither language nor meaning is a primarily human affair. Furthermore, both structuralism and phenomenology subordinate change and becoming to stasis and identity, assuming that what exists is individual fixed entities that only subsequently change or become something else. Structuralism can account for change only on the basis of static structures, and phenomenology can account for change only on the basis of a static first-person perspective. As we will shortly see, this is one of Deleuze's main problems with the Western tradition as a whole.

True to the outlook of the underground man, Deleuze sets out to show not that structuralism's language or phenomenology's first-person perspective is arbitrary, but that they are more enigmatic than we usually allow: they are not the firm and unshakable bedrock of knowledge that they are assumed to be, for there is indeed a "new logic" to be found, one that "grasps the innermost depths of life and death without leading us back" (*ECC*, 82) to fixed structures and a static, unitary first-person perspective. This new logic is that our structures of meaning and

8. This sketch of Deleuze's difference from structuralism is indebted to Colebrook, *Understanding Deleuze*, 28.

our sense of ourselves as stable points of view are effects of more fundamental forces and flows of desire that precede the human.

If Deleuze distances himself from the structuralism and phenomenology prevalent during his intellectually formative years, his thought also stands apart from others of his own generation (such as Derrida and Foucault) in important ways. Whereas Foucault the historian cares little for the ontology underlying the historical shifts he describes, and Derrida works studiously to avoid, as best he can, falling afoul of the violence of metaphysics, Deleuze unashamedly and enthusiastically embraces metaphysical themes and concepts. In a 1986 interview, he admits that "I've never been worried about going beyond metaphysics or any death of philosophy" (*Ne*, 88), which is just one of the ways in which Deleuze does not fit the caricature of a postmodern thinker. He rejects the characteristically postmodern determination to resist metaphysics with the dismissal that "the death of metaphysics or the overcoming of philosophy has never been a problem for us: it is just tiresome, idle chatter" (*WIP*, 9). Deleuze offers us an ontology, an account of being, and he does so unapologetically and without qualification.

One further factor to take into account when it comes to appreciating Deleuze's thought is that many of his best-known and most influential works written from 1972 to 1991 were coauthored with the psychotherapist Félix Guattari. It would be fruitless to seek to carve up books such as *A Thousand Plateaus* and *What Is Philosophy?* into Deleuzian and Guattarian influences, and we will engage in no such fool's errand in these pages.[9]

---

9. The working relationship between Deleuze and Guattari has frequently been described in terms of the complex interaction of the wasp and the orchid that they both discuss:

> Nothing would be gained by reducing a symbiosis like that of the wasp and the orchid to a simple "attachment" between two heterogeneous worlds. . . . The new symbiotic assemblage actually functions like a mutant wasp-orchid

Where appropriate, I will refer to "Deleuze and Guattari" rather than "Deleuze," but I will resist any further attempt to distinguish the sole-authored from the coauthored Deleuzian texts.

The Approach of This Book

In keeping with the pattern of the Great Thinkers series, the first half of this book will seek to give a faithful account of the main aspects of Deleuze's thought in his own terms. We cannot hope to bring Deleuze into conversation with Christian theology if we do not first seek to understand what he is saying. The three sections of this first half will deal with Deleuze's work in a roughly chronological sweep. First we address Deleuze's account of the *dogmatic image of thought* and his *reversal of Platonism*, a theme prominent in his earlier works, most notably *Difference and Repetition* (1968/1994) and *The Logic of Sense* (1969/1990).[10] We then turn to his rejection of the modern Cartesian subject in favor of the *body without organs* in *Anti-Oedipus* (1972/1977) and *A Thousand Plateaus* (1980/1987). Finally, we address political themes in Deleuze's later writing.

Each of these three sections looks first at how Deleuze understands the dominant way of thinking with which he disagrees (which he calls the *dogmatic image of thought*), before looking at

---

species evolving on its own account and redistributing the genetic and semiotic components selected from both original species according to its own standards. (Félix Guattari, *Lines of Flight: For Another World of Possibilities* [London: Bloomsbury, 2015], 202)

The Deleuze/Guattari relationship is treated in detail in François Dosse, *Gilles Deleuze and Félix Guattari: Intersecting Lives*, trans. Deborah Glassman (New York: Columbia University Press, 2011), and Ronald Bogue, *Deleuze and Guattari* (London: Routledge, 1989).

10. Where two dates are given, the first refers to the date of publication of the original French edition, and the second to the date of publication of the English translation.

his own position. This sequence is important for two reasons: first, because it helps us to understand why Deleuze says what he does, and why for him it is a very good thing to say what he does; second, because addressing the positions against which Deleuze argues makes strange some of the habits and practices that most of us take for granted most of the time, forcing us to consider why we think and act as we do.

There are, of course, great swaths of Deleuze's thought that I will leave relatively untouched in a volume of this length: his work on literature and the arts (Kafka, Proust, Bacon, cinema), his critique of capitalism, schizoanalysis, his book on Leibniz, and the argument of *What Is Philosophy?* I leave some areas of Deleuze's thought undiscussed in order that others can be explained and explored at greater length. This is a strategic decision with both benefits and costs. Readers seeking further explanation of areas about which I remain silent are encouraged to consult the bibliography at the end of this book, and some terms not discussed in the main text are also given brief definitions in the glossary.

In the second part of the book, I will attempt to bring Deleuze's thought into conversation with a range of biblical motifs that will, I hope, help us to understand both where Deleuze's thought and the Bible are at odds and where they make similar moves. This is a risky business. We can, of course, rest content to explain Deleuze to Deleuzians and the Bible to Christians, and there is indeed value in both those projects. But how much greater the challenge, how much more tantalizing and, perhaps, worthwhile it is to seek to explain Deleuze to a readership largely unfamiliar with, and in large part suspicious of, his thought, and to seek to explain aspects of the Bible in terms of a philosopher who in the main is predisposed to reject it and impute to it all manner of hypocritical motivations and evil implications.

PART 1

DELEUZE'S THOUGHT

In 1917 Marcel Duchamp purchased a "Bedfordshire" model porcelain urinal from a Manhattan ironworks, signed it "R. Mutt," dated it "1917," called it *Fountain*, and submitted it to the first exhibition of the American Society of Independent Artists as one of his now-famous "readymades." The piece has attracted

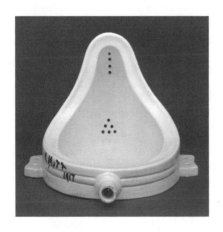

ridicule and adulation ever since, and in one 2004 BBC survey, *Fountain* was voted the most influential work of modern art.[1]

If *Fountain* is not to your artistic taste, then how

Fig. P1.1. Marcel Duchamp, Fountain (1917), replica 1964, Tate Gallery, London.[2]

1. http://news.bbc.co.uk/2/hi/entertainment/4059997.stm.
2. Source: https://commons.wikimedia.org/wiki/File:Marcel_Duchamp,_1917, _Fountain,_photograph_by_Alfred_Stieglitz.jpg . Public domain.

about Maxime Maufra's *Marée basse à la plage de Port Blanc, presqu'Île de Quiberon* (*Low Tide at the Beach at Port Blanc, Peninsula of Quiberon*), painted in the same year as Duchamp's urinal:

Fig. P1.2. Maxime Maufra, Marée basse à la plage de Port Blanc, presqu'Île de Quiberon (1917) private collection.[3]

Now let me ask you a question about these two works of art. Which is a better reflection of its time? Lest we need to be reminded, in 1917 Europe is plunged deep in one of the bloodiest wars in its history, with the mechanized slaughter of shells, gas, and machine guns tearing through the flesh of hundreds of thousands of the continent's youth. The first day of the battle of the Somme alone (July 1, 1916) saw 57,470 casualties and 19,240 dead. Which of these two works of art resonates more with the senseless, barbaric horror engulfing Europe—and, by 1917, the United States as well—at this time? Which resonates more with the crisis of traditional culture that it precipitated?

---

3. Source: https://www.the-athenaeum.org/art/list.php?s=tu&m=a&aid=392 &p=2. Public domain.

Maufra's canvas is as relevant to its geopolitical moment as organizing a poetry reading on the deck of the sinking *Titanic*: it may be a fine pursuit at another time and place, but it is not what the present circumstances call for. Duchamp's *Fountain*, by contrast, was created only three days after the United States declared war on Germany on April 6, 1917, and screams, as David Lubin has argued, an "'obscene' comment on the obscene nature of the war."[4] Context dictates what is relevant and required: We don't crack corny jokes at a funeral, any more than we expect a stand-up comic to sing funereal dirges. There is a time and place for Duchamp's *Fountain*, and 1917 in the bubble of the stuffy, self-congratulatory Manhattan art world was just that time and just that place.

The principle does not hold only for artworks. New wine needs to be poured into new wineskins: each historical moment has its own way of writing literature, its own way of dressing, of speaking. So why not its own way of philosophizing? What would a philosophy that reflected the Western world of the mid- to late twentieth century look like? What would its concerns and its concepts be? This is the very question that Gilles Deleuze addresses in a 1968 interview with Jean-Noel Vuarnet:

> Philosophy, too, must create worlds of thought, a whole new conception of thought, of "what it means to think," and it must be adequate to what is happening around us. It must adopt as its own those revolutions going on elsewhere, in other domains, or those that are being prepared. (*DI*, 138)

For Deleuze, the age of student uprisings, of sexual and social revolutions, needs its own way of thinking, just as 1917 needed its *Fountain*:

---

4. https://blog.oup.com/2017/05/marcel-duchamps-political-work-art/.

> We get the feeling that we can't go on writing philosophy
> books in the old style much longer; they no longer interest
> the students, they don't even interest their authors. So, I think
> everyone is on the look-out for something new. (*DI*, 141)

This is by no means a claim that philosophy should merely mirror its historical moment; in fact, for Deleuze, it is very important
indeed that philosophy "is always against its time" and a "critique
of the present world" (*NaP*, 107). To be a critique of the present world, however, is not the same as to be a critique of the
world of a century ago. It is with this idea, then, that we begin
our exploration of Deleuze's thought: He is seeking to fashion a
way of thinking that is appropriate to his time. And our opening
question is this: What might be the contours of a way of thinking
appropriate to late-twentieth-century Western society?

1

PLATO AND THE DOGMATIC IMAGE OF THOUGHT

What our historical moment demands, Deleuze argues, is not a handful of new ideas, but a new *image of thought*. This notion of an image of thought will be central for our engagement with Deleuze in this book. An image of thought is not *what* we think about; it is *how* we think about everything. It has distant affinities with what we call a *worldview*, but it is less about what we believe than how we believe everything we believe. It is not a list of doctrines but a set of assumptions about how knowledge works and what counts as *truth*. It is our image of thought that "determines our goals when we try to think" (*DR*, xvi), and that gives us a reason to think in the first place. Our image of thought is "implicit, subjective, and preconceptual" (*WIP*, 61); it encompasses our commitments that are so basic, we do not even consider them commitments but simply "the way things are" or "common sense." We might think of an image of thought as a computer operating system: not a particular app that allows the user to do this or that, but the software on which all such apps rely and that provides a platform for the user to do anything at all, all the while within the particular constraints of this or that operating system. An image of thought therefore precedes and grounds thought as the "prolegomena to philosophy" (*Ne*, 149).[1]

In order to better appreciate just what such an image of thought can look like, let us turn our attention to a particular example: the *dogmatic image of thought*, which, Deleuze argues, has controlled much of Western thinking for centuries and undergirds philosophical tendencies as diverse as empiricism and rationalism, and thinkers as varied as Plato, Descartes, Kant, and Heidegger (*DR*, 132). This "dogmatic," "orthodox," or "moral" image of thought (*DR*, 131) is addressed in a number of places in Deleuze's writings, though at greatest length in the third chapter of *Difference and Repetition* (*DR*, 129–67) and the second and third chapters of *What Is Philosophy?* (*WIP*, 35–84). Deleuze offers us both a threefold account of the dogmatic image (in *Nietzsche and Philosophy*) and an eightfold understanding (in *Difference and Repetition*). I will follow here the division into "three essential theses" (*NaP*, 103) of truth, error, and method. I will use Plato as a privileged example, for Deleuze understands him to be the originator and chief exponent of the dogmatic image (*DR*, 142).

Truth

Deleuze summarizes the place of truth in the dogmatic image of thought in terms of three principles (*NaP*, 103): (1) it is assumed that the thinker transparently and straightforwardly desires truth, (2) it is assumed that truth is straightforwardly

---

1. At one point, Deleuze uses the term *image of thought* to describe Foucault's historical epistemes: extended periods of time during which knowledge was constructed according to particular rules (*DI*, 92–93). For a more detailed explanation of Foucauldian epistemes, see chapter 1, "History and Truth," in my *Michel Foucault*, Great Thinkers (Phillipsburg, NJ: P&R Publishing, 2018).

what you reach if you think correctly, and (3) it is assumed that everyone can find truth by thinking if they follow their own will to truth. Yet this truth is to be found, according to the dogmatic image of thought, not within our immediate experience, but in a transcendent, abstract, and universal realm (*NaP*, 103–4) that needs to be interpreted by me, or disclosed or revealed to me.

This way of thinking about truth can be traced back to Plato, for "the poisoned gift of Platonism is to have introduced transcendence into philosophy, to have given transcendence a plausible philosophical meaning" (*ECC*, 137). For Plato, truth is to be found not in the world of our immediate sense experience (represented by the lower circle in the diagram below), but in another world, the world of what he calls the "Forms," eternal, unchanging archetypes of everything that exists in this world. These Forms can be apprehended only through our rational intellect, not through our senses (the upper circle). For example, we can express a perfect circle in a mathematical formula and understand it rationally, but we have never seen an absolutely perfect circle with our eyes.

Fig. 1.1. For Plato, truth is not found in this world but in the world of Forms, which can be apprehended only intellectually, not through the senses.

Something in this world is true if it faithfully (though never perfectly) copies one of the Forms and thereby—as Plato puts it—"participates" in it. So, for example, my wife's dear old childhood Labrador, Tammy, would, for Plato, participate in the perfect, eternal Form of the dog, and that relationship would constitute it as a "true" dog. If something participates in a Form in this way, for Plato it is an "icon" or good copy of that Form. Tammy the (imperfect) dog is an image of the eternal Form of the perfect dog. This is Plato's account of the relationship between Form (F) and true copy (c):

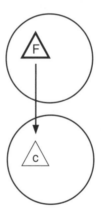

Fig. 1.2. An icon or good copy (c) is a faithful though imperfect reproduction of the eternal Form (F).

How do we come to know the truth of something? According to the dogmatic image of thought, we recognize that it is an icon of a Form. In other words, we relate it to a preestablished category; we say, "This (four-legged animal with a long, lolling tongue and eyes pleading for a treat) is that (a dog)." Recognition, then, does not create new ideas; it matches things in this world to preexisting—indeed, eternal—Forms. We might think of it, therefore, as a grand epistemological game of bingo:

I have to match the things I encounter in the world to the pre-existing categories I am given, and in this game there are only two options: either an object matches a Form or it does not. For Deleuze, this sort of recognition is central to the dogmatic image of thought from Plato through Descartes to Kant and beyond (*DR*, 134): to know the truth of something is to recognize its correspondence to a Form. What is recognized, however, is not only this correspondence of objects to Forms but also "the values attached to an object," such as the idea that a dog is a good companion and a faithful friend. This is because the language of our social and linguistic group signifies concepts that carve up the world in socially and practically valued ways. So when we say, "This is that," we are not so much recognizing the object as employing the valued way of categorizing things. This seems, perhaps, innocuous enough, but for Deleuze it "bears witness to a disturbing complacency" (*DR*, 135) because there is no room for me to question or challenge either the identity of the object or the values that attach to it.

Alongside this principle of recognition, the account of truth in the dogmatic image of thought relies on the idea of representation. According to the paradigm of representation, my thought is a mirror of the world. I am thinking truly when what is present out there in the world is accurately represented in my thoughts. Just like recognition, once more this makes truth-finding into a bingo game: either my thoughts accurately represent the stable reality with which I am presented or they do not.

In the paradigm of representation and recognition, sameness and identity are king. I begin with something stable and unchanging, whether the Platonic Form or a stable external reality. When there is difference, it is always a difference between two or more such stable Forms, with the consequence, as Deleuze dramatically puts it, that any radical difference that does not rely on such stable identities "is crucified" (*DR*, 138). This subordination of difference to identity is epitomized for Deleuze in what is known as *Porphyry's tree*, a way of classifying all living things on a hierarchical scale in terms of what they have in common. The two diagrams below show a pictorial representation of the tree, followed by a schema of its categories and relations:

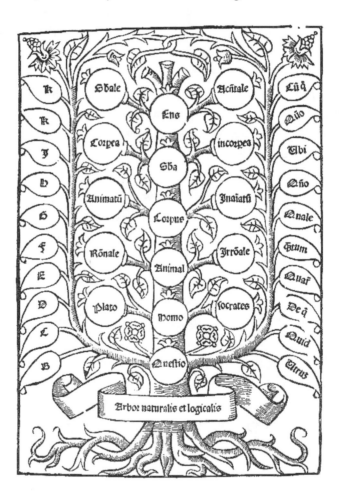

Fig. 1.3. Porphyry's Tree[2]

2. Source: https://en.wikipedia.org/wiki/Porphyrian_tree#/media/File: Porphyrian_Trees_Gallery_small.png . Public domain.

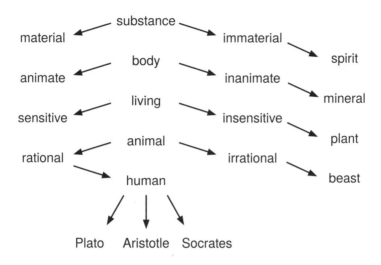

Fig. 1.4. Schematization of Porphyry's Tree

For the dogmatic image of thought and the Aristotle-inspired Porphyry's tree, identity precedes difference such that "only that which resembles differs" (*LS*, 261).

One final element of the account of truth in the dogmatic image of thought is its reliance on what Deleuze calls the "good will" of the truth-seeking thinker. This, too, is found in the Platonic dialogues, in which Socrates leads his interlocutors to the truth with nothing but his own questions and their good faith. A genuine desire to find truth, it is assumed, will always draw seekers nearer to their desired goal. This also requires, in addition to "a good will on the part of the thinker," that there be "an upright nature on the part of thought" (*DR*, 131). In other words, it requires the assumption that if we genuinely seek the true, it will not trick or deceive us. In fact, truth and goodness are inextricable for Plato: to find the truth, one must be of good will, and this good will must certainly be rewarded. This is part of what Deleuze means when he calls the dogmatic image of thought *moral*.

Error

The second of the three pillars of the dogmatic image of thought is its understanding of error:

> We are also told that we are "diverted" from the truth but by forces which are foreign to it (body, passions, sensuous interests). We fall into error, we take falsehood to be truth, because we are not merely thinking beings. Error: this would be merely the effect, in thought as such, of external forces which are opposed to thought. (*NaP*, 103)

The important point here is that for the dogmatic image of thought, error does not belong to thought itself or originate with the thinker; it is always ancillary forces that lead thinking astray. Every image of thought has something that it abominates, Deleuze argues (*WIP*, 54), and what the dogmatic image of thought abominates is error. Lots of things can go wrong for thought, including internal problems such as "stupidity, forgetfulness, aphasia, delirium, madness" (*WIP*, 52), and the "error" brought about by external causes.

When it comes to Plato's thought, error takes a particular name: *simulacrum*. In addition to the eternal, perfect Forms and the icons or faithful copies of those Forms, simulacra are false or unfaithful copies that, by contrast with icons, do not participate in the Forms. Plato's own example in his *Republic* is of a bed. First, there is the perfect, eternal Form of the bed (F). The carpenter's wooden bed, although not perfect, participates in the Form because it is, after all, a bed. It is a true copy (c)—a true image or a true imitation—of the Form of the bed, represented in the figure below by a line leading from Form to copy. An artist's painting of the carpenter's bed, by contrast, does not participate in the Form of a bed at all, because one cannot take one's night's rest in it. It gives the impression of being a true bed, but it is not. It is a false image. The carpenter's bed is an icon, but the artist's bed is a simulacrum (s) that does not participate in the Form of a bed.

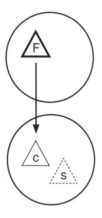

Fig. 1.5. In Plato's Republic, the carpenter's bed is a true copy (c) of the Form of the bed (F), but the artist's painting of a bed is a false copy, a simulacrum (s).

We might think that Plato begins with the Form, progresses to the icon, and finally identifies the simulacrum, rather as I have done in this explanation. For Deleuze, however, the order is exactly reversed. Plato begins with the problem of how to tell the true image from the false, how to tell the icon from the simulacrum, and invents the idea of the Form as a way to solve that problem. The problem of distinguishing true from false copies, furthermore, has political origins: icons are regular and predictable, and they conform to the Form in which they participate (see fig. 1.6), but simulacra represent an untamed potential for difference and instability that cannot be controlled and limited by any stable Form. The political equivalent to this is the sophist who, in Athenian democracy, could convince a crowd of anything through a persuasive use of rhetoric, regardless of whether he considered it true. Such an anarchic difference is a threat, then, not only to the stability of the Forms, but also to the stability of morals and a well-ordered society. This is why Deleuze claims that "the will to eliminate simulacra or phantasms has no motivation apart from the moral" (*DR*, 265) and that the nature of this moral motivation is a desire to preserve stability and order.

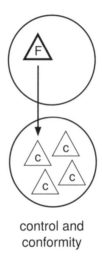

control and
conformity

Fig. 1.6. Refusing simulacra ensures conformity, predictability, and order.

To protect the stability of the state and traditional moral codes from attack by the anarchy of the sophist's whim, Plato creates the concept of an eternal and stable Form as a way to justify the difference between good and bad images, between icons and simulacra. In fact, "there is no State which does not need an image of thought which will serve as its axiomatic system or abstract machine, and to which it gives in return the strength to function" (*D*, 88), and Plato obliges by providing the authoritarian police state with a very effective image of thought. What a spectacularly successful creation the Platonic Form has been, described by Miguel de Beistegui as "the most formidable and arguably successful concept of the entire history of philosophy."[3] For Deleuze, then, Plato's ontology is political all the way down, and "with Platonism, philosophy becomes a police operation."[4]

Method

In addition to its particular understanding of truth and error, the dogmatic image of thought employs a particular method, as Deleuze explains:

> We are told, finally, that all we need to think well, to think truthfully, is a method. Method is an artifice but one through which we are brought back to the nature of thought, through which we adhere to this nature and ward off the effect of the alien forces which alter it and distract us. Through method we ward off error. Time and place matter little if we apply method: it enables us to enter the domain of "that which is valid for all times and places." (*NaP*, 103)

This idea of an infallible philosophical method that comes with a gold-plated guarantee to lead the thinker into the truth is most usually identified with René Descartes, who, in his *Discourse on the Method of Rightly Conducting One's Reason and of Seeking Truth in the Sciences*, employs the famous method of doubting all that is possible to doubt. This method of hyperbolic doubt leaves untouched only the existence of the thinking self because, even if I doubt, then I am thinking, and if I am thinking, then I exist. It is Plato's method, however, on which I want to focus here. Deleuze characterizes Plato's method in terms of division: "the selection

3. Miguel de Beistegui, "The Deleuzian Reversal of Platonism," in *The Cambridge Companion to Deleuze*, ed. Daniel W. Smith and Henry Somers-Hall (Cambridge: Cambridge University Press, 2012), 58.

4. De Beistegui, "Deleuzian Reversal of Platonism," 59.

among rivals, the testing of claimants" (*DR*, 60), with a view to dividing, both epistemologically and politically, the true from the false image, and then eliminating the simulacrum.

So in preparation for considering Deleuze's own philosophy, we can present the dogmatic image of thought in tabular form:

TRUTH	The true image: icon. Participation in the Form. Recognition and representation. Good will.
ERROR	The false image: simulacrum.
METHOD	Division.

Fig. 1.7. Summary of the Dogmatic Image of Thought

Ethics, Politics, and Theology of the Dogmatic Image of Thought

For Deleuze, the dogmatic image of thought has the philosophical consequences of obscuring the real role that difference plays in the genesis of thought and offering false conception of transcendence, but there are also grave ethical and political consequences that issue from our society's having lived under the dogmatic image of thought for so long. To begin with, recognition and representation crush creative thought. If our thinking amounts to matching what is in our head to what is in the world, and in matching objects to eternal categories, then how can we possibly think creatively and change society? Representation "mobilizes and moves nothing" (*DR*, 55–56), and the dogmatic image of thought is a recipe for perpetuating whatever injustices and inequalities currently exist. Such a privilege of identity over difference "profoundly betrays what it means to think" (*DR*,

167), and means that "philosophy is left without means to realize its project of breaking with doxa" (*DR*, 134), of breaking with
commonsense notions that everyone "knows" and no one thinks
to question.

Deleuze also sees the dogmatic image of thought as nihilistic
because it encourages us to put all our hope for truth and meaning in another, higher world, denying what truth and meaning
may otherwise have been ours in this world. When the higher
world proves inaccessible or we begin to lose faith in its existence, we are left with nothing, worse off than we were before
we renounced earthly pleasures in the name of something higher.
We are then condemned to live in the shadow of the world we
have lost, always feeling the gaping chasm of its absence. Like the
compulsion of the drug addict who can never hold on to a high
and is perpetually condemned to seek—and never to find—the
perfect trip, so also the addiction to transcendence condemns
the truth-addict to seek interminably for the higher world of
Forms even long after he knows that his cause is lost (*NaP*, 125).

Although Deleuze develops his account of the dogmatic
image of thought primarily in relation to Plato, it also structures his understanding of Christianity. Christian theology, for
Deleuze, places the "true" meaning of this world in an inaccessible transcendence, in this case the transcendence of God himself.
This leads to an ascetic renunciation of this world's pleasures
and ultimately issues in nihilism when we lose our confidence
in the existence of a higher world. God is the God of order, of a
hierarchical universe where everything should be in its proper
place and where the main task of judgment is to distinguish
the true from the false. God, for Deleuze, is "the master of the
exclusions and restrictions" (*AO*, 77), and just as Plato judges
images according to whether they participate in eternal Forms,
so in Deleuze's understanding of Christianity individuals are
judged on the basis of whether they are good copies (images)

or bad copies (simulacra) of Christ, the perfect image of God. The difference is that in the case of Christianity, failure to measure up to the divine image brings infinite debt and infinite guilt (see *ECC*, 126–35), a guilt and debt the feeling of which remains even after belief in the transcendent has been lost. Theologians, for their part, spend their time playing the Platonic game of distinguishing between "true" and "false" theological formulations. Deleuze approves of Nietzsche's famous quip that Christianity is "Platonism for the people."[5]

Deleuze's God is a judging God, and he often uses the phrase "the judgment of God" to summarize this emphasis. The reference is not primarily to the judgment of condemnation but to the judgment that imposes order, hierarchy, conformity, and stability: "the judgment of God is nothing other than the power to organize to infinity" (*ECC*, 130). Just like the Platonic method of division, the judgment of God "presupposes pre-existing criteria" and so "can neither apprehend what is new in an existing being nor even sense the creation of a mode of existence" (*ECC*, 134–35). Finally, the infinite judgment of God spawns a society of judgment in which individuals ape this divine characteristic by engaging in interminable ordering judgment of both themselves and others, thereby creating a regime of the strictest surveillance, order, and conformity.

Up until this point, I have been taking it for granted that Deleuze does not like the dogmatic image of thought. But there is a problem with the idea of condemning one image of thought from within another. Images of thought give us the criteria for deciding what is true and false, good and bad. How, then, can they themselves be better or worse than each other, any more

5. Friedrich Nietzsche, *Beyond Good and Evil: Prelude to a Philosophy of the Future*, ed. Rolf-Peter Horstmann and Judith Norman, trans. Judith Norman (Cambridge: Cambridge University Press, 2002), 4. The meaning of Nietzsche's phrase has not gone uncontested.

than baseball is "worse" than soccer simply because baseball players cannot score goals? It is a question asked by Deleuze himself
in *What Is Philosophy?*, in a passage where he is using the notion
of *planes of immanence* as a near-synonym for *images of thought*:

> Can we say that one plane is "better" than another or, at least,
> that it does or does not answer to the requirements of the age?
> What does answering to the requirements of the age mean,
> and what relationship is there between the movements or
> diagrammatic features of an image of thought and the move-
> ments or sociohistorical features of an age? (*WIP*, 58)

What is clear in Deleuze's ultimately inconclusive discussion
is that images of thought are not arbitrary. They do respond
to the "requirements of the age," whatever precise form that
response might take, and furthermore they "cannot arise in any
order whatever" because a new image of thought will develop,
change, break up, and conglomerate aspects of a previous image
(*WIP*, 58).

These two principles will guide us through our treatment of
Deleuze's alternative to the dogmatic image of thought below: its
relationship to that dogmatic image is complex, and it responds
to the requirements of its own age.

What does it mean, though, for an image of thought to
respond to the requirements of its age? In *Difference and
Repetition*, Deleuze characterizes the relationship in terms of a
shock: "Something in the world forces us to think" (*DR*, 139).
What we encounter in the world that forces us to think is not
a proposition but a certain imperceptible something "that can
only be sensed" (*DR*, 139), not recognized or represented. If
the political question to which Plato's philosophy is an answer is
"how can we ensure stability and order in the state?," for Deleuze,
the greatest question for philosophy is "how the production of

something new in the world is possible" (*2RM*, 344; cf. *DI*, 93). If we remember that Deleuze is writing in the midst of, and then in the wake of, the historical moment of the 1960s social revolutions, this indeed does appear as a pressing question of the time, which the events of the late 1960s force us to consider.

For Deleuze, we cannot hope to erect a new image of thought until we have critiqued the dogmatic image (*DR*, xiv). This critique of our existing image of thought is, in fact, a precondition of all real philosophy, for every great thinker renews the image of thought in some way: "we cannot imagine a great philosopher of whom it could not be said that he has changed what it means to think; he has 'thought differently' (as Foucault put it)" (*WIP*, 51). Concomitantly, Deleuze has little time for those who do not seek to renew the image of thought, whom he dismisses as "not philosophers but functionaries who, enjoying a ready-made thought, are not even conscious of the problem and are unaware even of the efforts of those they claim to take as their models" (*WIP*, 51).

What is called for, Deleuze argues, is not a new image of thought to replace the old, but a liberation from the idea that thought should follow the scripted pathways of an image at all. What he is seeking is "a liberation of thought from those images which imprison it" (*DR*, xvii). He offers us a positive account of what it means to think that foregrounds the role of "free difference" in the genesis of thinking and begins with an encounter with reality, rather than avoiding thought altogether by merely categorizing and "matching" the world to preexisting categories. This is a revolution in thought parallel to the revolution that led from representation to abstraction in art (*DR*, 276).

No one is more important for the critique of the dogmatic image of thought, or for elaborating a thought without image, than Friedrich Nietzsche. Nietzsche more than anyone else questions truths, "not because he wants to 'relativize' them like an ordinary skeptic" (*DI*, 135–36), for that would simply resolve to the "arbitrary" pole of the underground man's dilemma. Nietzsche's approach is more radical than relativizing truth; what matters is not truth but the sense of what one says and one's evaluation of one's own words, and "the categories of thought are not truth and falsity but the noble and the base, the high and the low" (*NaP*, 104).

Whereas Plato invents the concept of the Form, Nietzsche invents a series of concepts that subtend his thought: "forces," "value," "becoming," and "life" (*WIP*, 65). Whereas Plato has a vertical image of thought populated with Forms, copies, and the will to truth, Nietzsche has (as we will discuss below) eternal return and the infinite movements of the will to power (*WIP*, 65). Deleuze identifies other thinkers whose work similarly seeks to overturn the dogmatic image of thought: Hume, Bergson, and Proust (*DI*, 139), Artaud (*DR*, 147), and Foucault (*DI*, 92). What they all have in common is that they disrupt the dogmatic image of thought's threefold reliance on truth, falsity, and method; for each of these thinkers, "there's something extraordinary in the way they tell us: thinking means something else than what you believe" (*DI*, 139).

2

DELEUZE'S REVERSAL
OF PLATONISM

At the grand opening of the Millennium Bridge in London on June 10, 2000, its designers were heralding "an absolute statement of our capabilities at the beginning of the 21st century." The futuristic bridge had been tested far in excess of any likely maximum weight and wind speeds. As the engineers found out later that same day, however, what it had not been tested for was the rhythmic padding of hundreds of feet. The story of the bridge's infamous opening is told in an article in *Science Daily*:

> At first, the bridge was still. Then it began to sway, just slightly. Then, almost from one moment to the next, the wobble intensified. And suddenly, people were walking like tentative ice skaters: planting their feet wide, pushing out to the side with each step. Left, right, left, right, in near-perfect unison. The synchrony was utterly unintentional. But it was those unchoreographed footfalls . . . that were responsible for turning a $32 million design triumph into a very embarrassing

engineering quandary. The bridge was closed almost immediately.[1]

The problem was that the natural frequency of the bridge—
the rhythm at which it begins to oscillate without the need for
an external force and in an ever more accentuated manner—
was close to the rhythm of human walking. Once the bridge
started swaying, the pedestrians began marching in step to
counteract the sway, which rapidly amplified the effect. The
unsuspecting bridge crossers had found a way to use features
of the bridge's own design to stress and, if they had persisted,
to destroy it.

Deleuze's relationship to the philosophy of Plato is in some
respects like that of the pedestrians to the Millennium Bridge.
He does not seek to attack Plato's philosophy from the outside,
but takes advantage of the features of Plato's thought itself in
order to stress it to the point—and indeed beyond the point—
of fracture. Unlike the pedestrians on the Millennium Bridge,
however, Deleuze's attempt to destabilize Platonism is quite
deliberate.

Deleuze's *reversal* or *overturning*[2] of Platonism is by no
means a simple rejection of all of Plato's ideas. On the contrary,
in *Difference and Repetition* and *Logic of Sense*, Deleuze defines
his own philosophy explicitly in terms of Platonic concepts, in
particular the simulacrum. Those Platonic concepts he retains,
however, he also repurposes for his own ends: "The task of modern philosophy has been defined: to overturn Platonism. That
this overturning should conserve many Platonic characteristics
is not only inevitable but desirable" (*DR*, 59). Deleuze does not
claim to be the first to have contemplated overturning Platonism,

1. https://www.sciencedaily.com/releases/2005/11/051103080801.htm.
2. The French term is *renversement*, the meanings of which include "reversal,"
"inversion," and "overthrow."

nor does he claim that his own thought arrives out of the blue or makes arbitrary divisions. The main influences on the overturning of Platonism are Nietzsche and Plato himself.

Plato's problem, at least the problem of his dialogue *Sophist*, is that the distinction between the true copy (the philosopher: Socrates) and the simulacrum (the sophist) is never quite as clear-cut as we might expect. A character called the *Eleatic Stranger* has the role of distinguishing Socrates from his false imitators. Toward the end of the dialogue, the Stranger is almost undone by an argument "disputing whether there could be such a thing as a likeness or an image or an apparition at all,"[3] leading Deleuze to conclude:

> Among the most extraordinary pages in Plato, demonstrating the anti-Platonism at the heart of Platonism, are those which suggest that the different, the dissimilar, the unequal—in short, becoming—may well be not merely defects which affect copies like a ransom paid for their secondary character or a counterpart to their resemblance, but rather models themselves, terrifying models of the pseudos in which unfolds the power of the false. (*DR*, 128)

So if the seeds of Platonism's reversal are already present in the *Sophist*, how does Deleuze exploit its natural frequency to disrupt its privilege of identity, recognition, and representation? In other words, what does it mean to reverse Platonism? Succinctly, "overturning Platonism means denying the primacy of original over copy, of model over image; glorifying the reign of simulacra and reflections" (*DR*, 66). Deleuze presents this glorification in overtly political terms, as if the simulacra were storming

---

3. Christopher Rowe, ed., *Plato: Theaetetus and Sophist*, Cambridge Texts in the History of Philosophy (Cambridge: Cambridge University Press, 2015), 171.

the Bastille of the aristocratic icon as part of a bid "to make the simulacra rise and to affirm their rights among icons and copies" (*LS*, 262). How do the simulacra do this? By becoming real. The simulacrum, for Plato, is a copy without an original, and he considers it unreal because it bears no relationship to the perfect and eternal. But if everything is simulacrum, if no copy can lay claim to be an original, then the inventive, creative copying that characterizes the simulacrum becomes simply what there is, and "the very idea of a model or privileged position is challenged and overturned" (*DR*, 69). The transcendent relation of Form and true copy is replaced by an immanent and ever-proliferating movement from one simulacrum to another. The precedence of identity over difference is reversed: now, proliferating differences and multiplicities are primary, and they produce illusions of identity only as an aftereffect.

We can continue to trace the contours of Deleuze's reversal of Platonism in a series of comparisons with Plato and Aristotle:

- For Plato, identity is behind everything and grounds all differences, but for Deleuze, "difference is behind everything, but behind difference there is nothing" (*DR*, 57).
- For Plato, the essence of a thing is invariable and incorporeal Form, but for Deleuze, "essence is always difference" (*PS*, 75) because "difference is what constitutes being, what makes us conceive being" (*PS*, 41). A thing's essence is not what it happens to be at the moment, but its power to become.
- For Plato, the distinction between copy and simulacrum engenders the necessity of judging between good and bad copies, but for Deleuze, the simulacrum is no longer a second-class or illusory copy and Plato's need to judge between the true and the false is replaced with the affirmation of appearances. *True* and *false* now qualify

the problem—the very idea that icons need to be distinguished from simulacra—rather than the relationship between image and reality itself.

- Furthermore, Deleuze calls the system of strict order and the policing of the difference between true and false copies the "judgment of God," but his own paradigm of simulacra takes a devilish name: "the system of the Antichrist is the system of simulacra opposed to the world of identities" (*LS*, 298).
- For Aristotle, "only that which resembles differs," but for Deleuze's overturning of Platonism, "only differences can resemble each other" (*LS*, 261).

It is not simply the case, however, that Deleuze straightforwardly replaces the Platonic primacy of identity with his own primacy of difference. Difference does not anchor and structure Deleuze's metaphysics in the same way that identity does Plato's, because whereas identity controls, judges, and polices, difference is a power of unfettered creation. We always already know what identity is; to say that essence is identity fixes and controls it. But to say that essence is difference gives us no sense of, or control over, what sorts of proliferating differences may eventuate in the future. To say that essence is identity is a gesture of prediction and control; to say that essence is difference is to lose control and the ability to predict what things may become. Identity names what we know; difference names what escapes our knowledge.

Having sketched some of the main contours of Deleuze's reversal of Platonism, we will now explore his thought in more detail. Deleuze engages with many philosophers and authors, as well as with some scientists, but three interlocutors stand head and shoulders above the rest in terms of their importance for Deleuzian philosophy: Baruch Spinoza, Henri Bergson, and Friedrich Nietzsche. We will now trace three of the main concepts in Deleuze's thought in relation to these three inter-locutors: Spinoza and immanence, Bergson and the virtual, and Nietzsche and eternal return.[4]

Spinoza and Immanence

For Deleuze, no philosopher contributes more to the good news of the overturning of Platonism than Baruch Spinoza (1632–77), the "Christ of philosophers" (*WIP*, 60). Spinoza's message is a gospel of immanence. Just as Christ "was incarnated once, in order to show, that one time, the possibility of the impossible," so also Spinoza conceived, once and for all, what Deleuze and Guattari call the *plane of immanence* (*WIP*, 59–60), a term that we will discuss below. Compared to this epochal contribution to philosophy, "the greatest philosophers are hardly more than apostles who distance themselves or draw near this mystery" (*WIP*, 60). Spinoza is also, along with Nietzsche, one of only two thinkers on whom Deleuze wrote two books: his *Expressionism in Philosophy: Spinoza* (1968/1990), originally the minor thesis of his Agrégation qualification, and *Spinoza: Practical Philosophy* (1970/1988).

It is Spinoza, then, who overcomes philosophy's addiction to transcendence. What distinguishes Spinoza for Deleuze is not merely the fact of his opposition to transcendence but its zeal; his thought denounces "all that separates us from life, all these transcendent values that are turned against life" (*SPP*, 26). Deleuze hails Spinoza as "the only philosopher never to have compromised with transcendence and to have hunted it down everywhere" (*WIP*, 48). His thought is therefore an antidote to

---

4. I am not suggesting that only Spinoza helps Deleuze to think immanence, only Bergson difference, and only Nietzsche eternal return. The threefold division should be seen as three perspectives on the same multifaceted philosophy, not three atomized ideas.

the nihilism, guilt, and judgment of God that attend philosophies of transcendence.

Univocity

So how did Spinoza so comprehensively overcome transcendence in philosophy, and how does Deleuze make use of this victory? One of the major planks of Spinoza's banishing of transcendence from philosophy is his insistence on the *univocity of being*. The tradition of Western philosophy has given us three main ways to understand being: equivocity, univocity, and analogy.

- Equivocity of being: There are different types of being that have no common measure between them. For example, when we say that God "is," we mean something incommensurably different from saying that a person or a stone "is." God's being is eternal and perfect, whereas the being of creation is temporal and imperfect. Another example is Descartes' substance dualism, which holds that there exist two fundamental substances: minds and bodies.
- Univocity of being: *Being* always means the same thing, no matter whether we are talking about God, minds, bodies, ideas, or rocks. If being is univocal in this way, then there can be no transcendence in the way traditionally understood in Christian theology.
- Analogy of being: Like equivocity, analogy holds that there are different types of being. Where analogy differs from equivocity, however, is that there is, precisely, an analogy between God's being and the being of creation, as there also is between God's communicable attributes and attributes of created things. "My brother is wise" and "God is wise" do not use the adjective *wise* in a univocal sense, but neither is it the case that the two statements

have nothing at all in common. God is wise without limit, and my brother is wise in a very imperfect way, but there is nevertheless a proportion or analogy between the two examples of wisdom. In the same way, "God is" and "my brother is" are neither univocal nor equivocal, but imply a relationship of analogy between God's perfect, uncreated being and my brother's finite, created being.

Deleuze dismisses equivocity as the royal road to transcendence, to a God whose being is unreachably beyond our own. As for analogy, he considers it an uncommitted halfway house that seeks to maintain the transcendence of equivocity but lacks the full courage of its convictions.[5] Univocity, by contrast, is attractive to Deleuze because it insists on "the equality of all forms of being" (*EPS*, 167). God is stripped of any transcendence and, for Spinoza, becomes ultimately indistinguishable from the natural world, giving rise to Spinoza's famous *deus sive natura* ("God or nature").

But if, as Spinoza maintains, "being . . . is said in a single same sense throughout all its forms" (*DR*, 304), then how can we account for the differences between beings? Does it not follow from univocity that all beings are, in the final analysis, the same being? Deleuze's response to this problem is not to attenuate univocity but to build on Spinoza's own explanation of difference in terms of being expressing itself differently in different "modes" of being, different entities in the world. Crucially, though, he dispenses with Spinoza's own insistence on a single substance and on his *deus sive natura*. Instead, Deleuze redefines being as difference. For Deleuze, to be is to differentiate: "Being is said in

5. Deleuze makes this judgment on analogy in his lecture at the University of Vincennes on January 14, 1974, available in English translation at https://www.web deleuze.com/textes/176. We will see in part 2 that this quick dismissal of analogy is challenged by not a few Christian responses to Deleuze's work.

a single and same sense of everything of which it is said, but that of which it is said differs: it is said of difference itself" (*DR*, 36).

This identification of being with difference means that, far from univocity's being a recipe for the ultimate identity of all things, it becomes a guarantee of variance and dissimilarity. We can go further than this, however. Univocity does not simply accommodate difference; it is for Deleuze the only possible guarantee of radical difference. If essences are identities, then differences can only ever be secondary qualities of those identities, and the secondary qualities are less real than the primary essences. But if essence is difference, then nothing is more real than differences, and all differences are just as fully real as each other. Furthermore, there is no being in general, for each difference is unique and cannot stand apart from or above other differences, acting like a Platonic Form. Deleuze and Guattari express this position in two lapidary formulas: "A single voice raises the clamor of being" (*DR*, 35), and "PLURALISM = MONISM" (*ATP*, 20).

Difference, for Deleuze, is so ubiquitous and so radical that we cannot hope to perceive it in all its proliferation. In order to perceive anything at all in the world, we need to reduce its difference, to slow its becoming down long enough to make it recognizable. Claire Colebrook helpfully illustrates Deleuze's point about the imperceptibility of radical difference with reference to the color spectrum: "When we perceive the difference between red and blue we do so only because we do not perceive the difference of each vibration of light; our eye contracts complex data into a single shade or object of red or blue."[6] We can perceive red and blue only after we have dramatically reduced the differences within those two broad categories. Perception is a filter that dampens down, selects, and limits the differences of the stimuli to which

6. Claire Colebrook, *Understanding Deleuze* (Sydney: Allen and Unwin, 2003), 28.

we respond. This once more sets Deleuze's thought at odds with prominent currents in much twentieth-century linguistic philosophy. Whereas for the structuralism of Saussure our language creates and introduces differences into the undifferentiated flux of reality, for Deleuze our language and concepts serve to reduce reality's overwhelming differences.

Plane of Immanence

In Deleuze's later work (*ATP, WIP*), he and Guattari distance themselves from the language of univocity and evoke instead what they call the *plane of immanence*.[7] This change in vocabulary emphasizes the rejection of Spinoza's idea of a single substance in favor of essence as difference. The idea of a plane of immanence is close to that of an image of thought. The plane of immanence contains all the principles and assumptions, all the concepts and relationships, that govern our thought and action. It is a plane of *immanence* because there is no transcendent God or substance to organize the differentiating and becoming of everything that is, and the notion of a flat *plane* emphasizes that there are no hierarchies in being: no instance of difference has more or less being than any other.

We must not think of the plane of immanence as a Platonic ontology lacking the Forms (see fig. 2.1). This is a picture of nihilism for Deleuze, not of his own thought. The plane of immanence, by contrast, is not Plato's system without the world of the transcendent Forms, but is complete in itself (see fig. 2.2).

The plane of immanence gives Deleuze what has been called a *flat ontology*,[8] in which there is no hierarchy between different degrees or types of being. Platonic metaphysics proliferates

7. Or the *plane of consistency*, a term used very frequently in *A Thousand Plateaus*.

8. *Flat ontology* is a term derived from the work of Manuel DeLanda, and Deleuze does not use it himself, though in *A Thousand Plateaus* he does mention *flat multiplicities*. The term appears in a number of commentaries on Deleuze's thought.

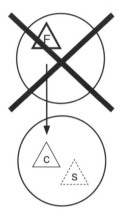

Fig. 2.1. Deleuze's reversal of Platonism should not be understood as Plato minus the world of the Forms.

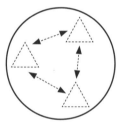

Fig. 2.2. The plane of immanence is not lacking Platonic Forms. It is complete in itself.

hierarchies of being: God is more real than creation, the present is more real than the past and the future, experience is more real than memory, objects are more real than ideas, facts are more real than fictions. But none of these differences introduce any hierarchy into being for Deleuze. In place of Platonic hierarchies, Deleuze and Guattari speak of *crowned anarchies* or nonhierarchical distributions of entities (*DR*, 278, 304).

In *A Thousand Plateaus*, Deleuze and Guattari express this flat ontology through the logic of the nonhierarchical conjunction *and*: There are objects and ideas and the present and the past and gods and monsters and atoms and ideas and universals and particulars and language and things and fictions and facts and thought and consciousness and bodies and experience and memory—all on the same plane of immanence, all existing with the same degree of reality, all expressions of essential difference. There may still emerge local, temporary hierarchies within the plane of immanence, but such hierarchies are no longer based on any criteria exterior to the beings on the plane, such as fundamental differences in their degree of being.

One particularly striking example of this flat ontology is Deleuze and Guattari's claim that "God is a lobster" (*ATP*, 4). There is no doubt in part a subversive, irreverent tone to this affirmation, but it also expresses something important about univocity and the plane of immanence. God, for Deleuze, is part of what there is, with just as much reality as anything else, including a lobster. With his "God is a lobster," Deleuze is also making a point about the function of God as a dispenser of judgments and creator of hierarchies and distinctions between the true and the false. The lobster's two pincers are in part an image of pinching and holding things together in conformity with stable categories, distinctions, and divisions.

Bergson and the Virtual

The second of our three key notions in Deleuze's thought emerges from his engagement with the early-twentieth-century French philosopher Henri Bergson (1859–1941). Whereas Spinoza helped Deleuze to arrive at a new understanding of immanence, through Bergson he rethinks time and existence.

Deleuze characterizes the traditional Western understanding of time as *linear*, *extensive*, and *spatialized*. It is linear because we imagine time progressing in a single line from the past through the present to the future. It is extensive because we imagine the line of past-present-future to be composed of many infinitesimally tiny and nonoverlapping "nows" through which the line extends in both directions. It is spatial because this model represents movement through time in terms of movement in space along a line. In this model, time is imagined as a spatial container that can be either full or empty: it still exists even if there are no events to fill it. Finally, this model of time privileges the present over the past and the future. The past exists only as memory and the future does not yet exist; only the present can truly be said to exist.

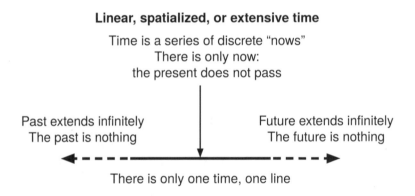

Linear, spatialized, or extensive time

Time is a series of discrete "nows"
There is only now:
the present does not pass

Past extends infinitely
The past is nothing

Future extends infinitely
The future is nothing

There is only one time, one line

Fig. 2.3. Linear, Spatialized, or Extensive Time

Duration

Across a series of books,[9] Bergson elaborates a radically different understanding of time, not as extension but as *duration* (French: *durée*). In the spatialized conception of time, the present is what it is because it is not past or future, but for Bergson's

9. See in particular *Time and Free Will: An Essay on the Immediate Data of Consciousness*, trans. F. L. Pogson (1889; repr., Whitefish, MT: Kessinger, 2010); *Duration and Simultaneity*, ed. Robin Durie (1922; repr., Manchester: Clinamen Press, 1999); *The Creative Mind*, trans. Mabelle L. Andison (1934; repr., New York: Citadel Press, 1946).

duration, present and past are inextricable from each other. To understand what Bergson and Deleuze mean, let us begin right where we are. I am currently sitting at a computer, typing this sentence. I can see the keys and screen in front of me, with a mug of coffee to my right, and a lemon tree outside the window in front of me. Or rather, I can see particular patches of color and shade, which I assume to be part of some larger things— the mug, the keyboard, the tree—only part of which I can see. Let's take the mug. How do I know that it is a mug, not just a surface? How, so to speak, do I know what is on the "dark side of the mug"? Well, I have drunk from it before, I brought it here from the kitchen a few minutes ago, and it looks like many other mugs I have seen in my life. In other words, my past experience of mugs is folded into my current perception, and the two work seamlessly together to form my experience of this mug before me. Without the past, there is no "mug" right here and right now. But it is not only my past experience of mugs that constitutes my present experience of this mug; everything that I have experienced in the past brings itself to bear on shaping my appreciation of the beauty, usefulness, physicality, temperature, economic value, and so forth of this mug.

In his book *Bergsonism*, Deleuze reproduces a series of diagrams from Bergson's *Matter and Memory* that help in understanding his notion of time. The diagrams feature an inverted cone SAB and a plane P. In the first diagram below (see fig. 2.4), the cone represents "the totality of the recollections accumulated in my memory," and the tip of the cone S touching the plane is the present. The plane itself is "my current representation of the universe."[10]

10. Henri Bergson, *Matter and Memory*, trans. N. M. Paul and W. S. Palmer (New York: Zone Books, 1988), 152, translation altered. Bergson's *représentation actuelle*, translated as "actual representation" in the English edition, should be correctly translated "current representation."

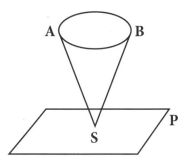

Fig. 2.4. Bergson's Model of Memory and Representation

Bergson calls "contraction" the fact that all my past memories are brought to bear on my experience of the present moment. My past experiences are contracted into my present experience at different speeds, however. Sometimes, when I take the time to contemplate something at leisure, my memories are more spread out and expanded; I may remember a particular time when I used this same mug, or I may remember how cold and heavy it feels in my hands when empty. Bergson represents these more reflective experiences with a circle of larger circumference: AB or A′B′ in the second figure below (see fig. 2.5). At other times, however (say when I knock the mug off my desk and have to respond quickly and try to catch it before it breaks on the

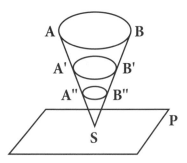

Fig. 2.5. Expansion and Contraction in Bergson's Model of Memory and Representation

floor), all my images and memories are still present in my actions to save the mug, but in a much more contracted way, represented by the point labeled S. The more physical and less contemplative my experience is, the closer it will be to the tip of the cone.

It is not that there are more memories in the larger cross-sections of the cone, but that the same memories are more expanded (*B*, 60). Furthermore, this contraction of the past is not linear. It does not take me four times as long to remember something that happened a month ago as it does to remember something that happened a week ago. Memories from my early childhood can coexist with memories from yesterday, without being "further away" in memory.[11] Past experience and present apprehension cannot be separated for Bergson, and "practically we perceive only the past, the pure present being the invisible progress of the past gnawing into the future."[12] As for Deleuze himself, he sums up the Bergsonian understanding of time in the following way:

> The past and the present do not denote two successive moments, but two elements which coexist: One is the present, which does not cease to pass, and the other is the past, which does not cease to be but through which all presents pass. . . . The past does not follow the present, but on the contrary, is presupposed by it as the pure condition without which it would not pass. (*B*, 59)

One further influence on Deleuze from Bergson's account of time is that the past has an ontological, not merely a psychological, existence. Bergson's reasoning goes like this: If the past were purely psychological, existing only in my and your subjective

11. This is one of the insights that Deleuze draws from Marcel Proust, who is also influential in his thinking about memory. See *PS*.

12. Bergson, *Matter and Memory*, 150.

recollections, then there would be as many pasts as there are people to recall them. But this is not the case; there is one common past, which "exists outside of consciousness, in time" (*C2*, 80). If this sounds a little strange, just think about space. We have no problem accepting that there are real objects in space even if we happen not to perceive them; why, Bergson argues, should it be any harder for us to see that there are real recollections in time even if we do not personally remember them?

Finally, Deleuze insists that time is intensive rather than extensive, and that therefore it is plural. Extensive time, it will be remembered, is time as a series of "nows" extending infinitely into the past and the future. But for Deleuze, this is committing in terms of time the same error that Plato makes in relation to essences: Plato abstracts supposedly eternal essences from the flow of becoming, and extensive time abstracts supposedly discrete "nows" from the flow of time that is always composed of memories and predictions. In contrast to this extensive account of time, Deleuze insists that time is intensive, by which he means that it is composed of durations drawing on retentions (memories) and protentions (intended actions, predictions). If we accept this view of time, it is clear that different organisms will experience different times. Animals with a greater capacity to remember and project into the future will have a longer duration than those without such capacities. One important implication of Bergsonian time, therefore, is that it is not anthropocentric. Human time has certain duration, but it is not the only or even the predominant duration in the world.

The Actual and the Virtual

In the same way that Deleuze develops and builds on Spinoza's univocity with his own concept of the plane of immanence, he also develops Bergsonian duration into his account of the actual and the virtual, a distinction already present in

Bergson's *Matter and Memory* but developed heavily by Deleuze. In Deleuze's hands, the actual/virtual distinction yields an understanding not only of memory but of the whole of reality. The virtual is one of the key concepts in Deleuze's thought, and one of the hardest to understand. Let us try to come to terms with it by considering ten propositions.

The Virtual Is Not the Possible

Deleuze insists most adamantly that the virtual is not the possible. In *Creative Evolution*, Bergson argues that Western metaphysics has traditionally distinguished between real and possible existence. To exist possibly is less than to exist really, in the same way that a possible $10 bill in my wallet is worth less to me than a real one. Following Bergson's argument in *The Creative Mind*, Deleuze argues in *Bergsonism* (96–98) that our traditional notion of the possible is in fact the real minus its existence and then projected back in time before real existence. One major problem with the concept of the possible for Deleuze is that what is real acts as a limit to and control on what is possible, just as Platonic ideas act as a limit to and control on true copies.

The Virtual Is Real

The possible, of course, is not real. A possible $10 bill in my wallet does not exist. This is not the case, by contrast, with the virtual. The virtual is no less real than the actual, any more than the "dark side of the mug" is less real than the side I can see. "The virtual is fully real in so far as it is virtual" (*DR*, 208), insists Deleuze, and the actual and the virtual together constitute the real, comprising two "unequal odd sides" or "dissimilar halves" of reality (*DR*, 209–10). The insistence that actual and virtual together constitute the real is one of the consequences of the univocity of being, for if there is only one sort of being, then the actual and the virtual must both exist in the same way.

The Virtual Is Pure Becoming and Variation

So what, then, is the virtual, if it is real but not actual? Deleuze describes it as a chaotic realm of pure becoming and variation and calls it *multiplicity*—not a multiple *of* anything, but "a pure multiplicity in the Idea which radically excludes the identical as a prior condition" (*DR*, 211–12). This multiplicity is not in opposition to unity or to the one, because, as we have already seen, identity is a product of difference for Deleuze. It is not the case that multiples emerge in the coming together of preexisting identities; on the contrary, identities emerge only when multiplicities slow down.

The Actual Is Pure Identity

By contrast with the pure becoming of multiplicity, the actual is characterized by fixed identity. It is the state of identifiable objects existing in linear time and geometric space. Differentiated parts, distinct individuals, and organized groups are all actual. Whereas Plato reserved eternal stability for the Forms, for Deleuze relative stability belongs to the realm of the actual.

The Difference between the Virtual and the Actual Is One of Speed

If the virtual and the actual are not distinguished in terms of their reality, then what differentiates them? The answer is speed. The virtual moves at an infinite speed: its differences and becomings are imperceptibly swift, which means that it can never be apprehended directly. In the actual, by contrast, these imperceptibly fast velocities are slowed down, creating what appear to be stable identities. We might think of the example of honey. When heated, honey flows much like water, but cooled down to room temperature it is much more viscous, retaining its shape for a moment as it is poured out or even crystallizing into a solid. Similarly, the actual actualizes various parts of the virtual (various differential relations) at different speeds, allowing it to retain its shape long enough for us to assign it an identity or an essence. Pure actuality—if you will pardon my straining the analogy—would be like frozen honey: its flow arrested into a rigid form. In both cases, the difference is one of speed. The honey illustration also has the virtue of showing that the actual and the virtual are not two different substances, like Plato's Forms and copies.

The Virtual Is Actualized

Whereas the possible is realized or made real, for Deleuze and Bergson the virtual is actualized. *Actualization* (or sometimes *differenciation*) describes the process by which differences and distinctions are made perceptible at different speeds. Deleuze explains actualization by using the example of the egg. There are "actualising, differenciating agencies" at work everywhere, he claims, but they are usually hidden by already-existing identities and qualities. We can glimpse, them, however, in the egg:

> Embryology shows that the division of an egg into parts is secondary in relation to more significant morphogenetic movements: the augmentation of free surfaces, stretching of cellular layers, invagination by folding, regional displacement of groups. A whole kinematics of the egg appears, which implies a dynamic. Moreover, this dynamic expresses something ideal. . . . Types of egg are therefore distinguished by the orientations, the axes of development, the differential speeds and rhythms which are the primary factors in the actualization of a structure and create a space and a time peculiar to that which is actualized. (*DI*, 214)

The structure of the egg in its transformation into an animal is an actualization of imperceptible differences present in the egg itself. The actual, then, is not a copy of the virtual on the pattern of Plato's Forms and copies, but a slowing down, selecting, and ossifying of some of its acutely complex and diverse differences to the point at which it becomes perceptible.

The Virtual Is More than the Actual

Whereas, according to the traditional schema of the real and the possible, the possible is less than the real, in Bergson and Deleuze's virtual/actual distinction, the virtual is more than the actual. This is because actualization must necessarily slow down the virtual, limiting its difference and its possibilities of becoming.

Pure Virtuality and Actuality Are Limits toward Which Things Tend

We should not think that the real is always either pure virtuality or pure actuality, either moving with infinite velocity or in complete stasis. Pure virtuality and pure actuality are limits toward which things tend, not a switch that has only two positions and nothing in between. Even the most stable objects or ideas are still not absolutely fixed and unchanging, and even the greatest velocity of becoming that we can perceive has not reached infinite speed. The diagram below (see fig. 2.6) represents entities at varying degrees of virtuality and actuality: from the imperceptibly swift becoming of the virtual to the rigid stasis approaching the actual.

We can represent the pure virtual as a uniform gray, not because it is undifferentiated but because its becomings and structure are moving too fast for us to discern them. We can represent the pure actual as a system of fixed identities, black dots on a white background. Between these two extremes, things are always tending in one direction or another, either to increased fixity or to increased becoming.

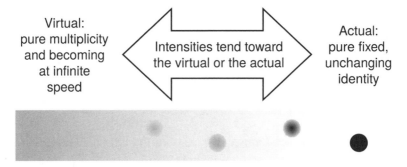

Fig. 2.6. Actuality and virtuality are states toward which things tend, not fixed categories like Plato's Forms and copies.

When the Virtual Slows Down Sufficiently, It Can Be Given a Name

In *A Thousand Plateaus*, Deleuze and Guattari discuss actualization by using the example of a hurricane. The hurricane itself is an unstable complex of differences in air temperature and changes in wind speed and direction that has no definite borders and no strict beginning and end in time, to which we have sought to attach a proper name as if it had a stable identity.

> The proper name does not indicate a subject; nor does a noun take on the value of a proper name as a function of a form or a species. The proper name fundamentally designates something that is of the order of the event, of becoming . . . . It is the military men and meteorologists who hold the secret of proper names, when they give them to a strategic operation or a hurricane. (*ATP*, 264)

For Deleuze and Guattari, all identities and all proper names share these features that are seen particularly clearly in the example of the hurricane. What we call *human beings*, for Deleuze, are merely a snapshot, taken at a particular historical moment, of an unbroken flow of evolution that began with single-celled organisms, that developed through fish, land animals, and primates, and that, if we survive long enough, will continue on beyond what is recognizably "human." Human beings are not as real as the flow of becoming of which they are a transient stage, or, as Todd May puts it, "the only being is the being of becoming."[13]

The Virtual Is the Transcendental Condition of Our Perception
Finally, we might ask how Deleuze can know so much about the virtual, if he has never encountered pure virtuality face to face, precisely because it cannot be apprehended face to face. As James Williams argues,[14] his response would be that unless we assume the virtual as the transcendental condition of the actual—as that without which the actual could not be what it is—we can offer no convincing account of how things are. In *Difference and Repetition*, Deleuze describes his thought as a *transcendental empiricism*. This has nothing to do with transcendence, for which we have seen Deleuze reserves only hatred. *Transcendental* here refers to the conditions of real experience (as opposed to Kant, whose transcendental inquiry searches for the condition of *possible* experience): what must being be like to give us the sort of world we experience?

Nietzsche and Eternal Return

The third major influence on Deleuze's thought is Friedrich Nietzsche and his concept of eternal return or eternal recurrence,

13. Todd May, *Gilles Deleuze: An Introduction* (Cambridge: Cambridge University Press, 2005), 60.

14. "[Deleuze] attempts to show that philosophies based purely on the actual or purely on identification miss and suppress virtual pre-conditions for their own arguments. He studies actual sensations in order to deduce these transcendental conditions and he argues that a failure to account for such conditions gives an incomplete view of any actual thing." James Williams, *Gilles Deleuze's* Difference and Repetition: *A Critical Introduction and Guide* (Edinburgh: Edinburgh University Press, 2003), 241.

which plays an important role in both Deleuze's ontology and his ethics. Nietzsche presents the idea of eternal return in *The Gay Science*:

> What if some day or night a demon were to steal into your loneliest loneliness and say to you: "This life as you now live it and have lived it you will have to live once again and innumerable times again; and there will be nothing new in it, but every pain and every joy and every thought and sigh and everything unspeakably small or great in your life must return to you, and in the same succession and sequence—even this spider and this moonlight between the trees, and even this moment and I myself. The eternal hourglass of existence is turned over again and again, and you with it, speck of dust!" Would you not throw yourself down and gnash your teeth and curse the demon who spoke thus? Or have you once experienced a tremendous moment when you would have answered him: "You are a god, and never have I heard anything more divine." If this thought gained power over you, as you are it would transform and possibly crush you; the question in each and everything, "Do you want this again and innumerable times again?" would lay on your actions the heaviest weight! Or how well disposed would you have to become to yourself and to life to long for nothing more fervently than for this ultimate eternal confirmation and seal?[15]

What this proposal accomplishes for Nietzsche is to give gravity to our actions without having to appeal to a divine judge, or even to transcendence at all (the demon is merely a device; what Deleuze takes from Nietzsche is the idea of a return that makes

15. Bernard Williams, ed., *Nietzsche: The Gay Science: With a Prelude in German Rhymes and an Appendix of Songs* (Cambridge: Cambridge University Press, 2001), 194–95.

no appeal to transcendence). Eternal return requires no metaphysical difference between this world and another; it introduces a notion of eternity that does not diminish but rather ennobles this life.

Deleuze's appropriation of this Nietzschean doctrine of eternal return has further important features, and his own account of eternal return is markedly different from Nietzsche's, just as he develops Spinozan univocity into the plane of immanence and Bergsonian duration into the actual/virtual distinction. For Deleuze, what returns are emphatically not past events exactly as they happened, and indeed "every time we interpret the eternal return as the return of the identical or the same, we replace Nietzsche's thought with childish hypotheses" (*NaP*, xi). What returns is, to be sure, everything there is, but we must remember from the discussion of Spinoza above that what there is, for Deleuze, is difference and becoming. The eternal return of all past events is, for Deleuze, the eternal return of the virtual difference and becoming from which those events were actualized, not the return of the actualized identities themselves: "Return is the being of that which becomes. Return is the being of becoming itself, the being which is affirmed in becoming" (*NaP*, 24). True repetition is a repetition of difference, and what returns is always the same only insofar as it is always different.

In order to see more clearly what Deleuze means, let us take an event: the invention of the steam engine. What will return is not the invention of the steam engine itself, as if a new James Watt needed to draw up the plans all over again, but the difference from previous means of harnessing power that it brought about. How do we repeat the event of the invention of the steam engine today? Not by inventing the steam engine again, but by producing a change to the current way we conceive the possibilities of transport of the same magnitude as that produced by Watt's invention. Or take a second example: Will the Beatles return? Not in the sense of John, Paul, George, and Ringo re-forming, no, but that is not the sort of return Deleuze means. What will return is the difference the Beatles made to the extant music scene: the newness of the sound, the innovation in lyrics, in instrumentation, and in presentation. So "the eternal return is linked, not to a repetition of the same, but on the contrary, to a transmutation" (*NaP*, xxi), to an affirmation of difference itself that will always produce different results. In fact, if something resembles past events, it is a sure sign that it is not a repetition of them, for "the most exact, the most strict repetition has as its correlate the maximum of difference" (*DR*, xxii).

The second important point to note about Deleuze's account of eternal return is that not everything returns. What does not return is "that which denies eternal return, that which does not pass the test" of difference, namely, "the identical, the similar and the equal, in so far as these constitute the forms of indifference" (*DR*, 243). Again, this follows from Deleuze's identification of being with difference. If what returns is difference, then the identical cannot return. Furthermore, given that difference and becoming are productive of life for Deleuze, the return of difference is an affirmation of life here and now, as opposed to life in the future and in a transcendent realm.

One further important consequence of eternal return for Deleuze is that it forecloses the possibility of the traditional Christian God in its "parodic reversal of Christian metaphysics."[16] Compared to eternal return, Deleuze dismisses the one-off transformation of Christian resurrection. In *The Logic of Sense*, Deleuze argues that the alternative to Nietzsche's eternal return is the sort of Christian return to be found in the writings of Kierkegaard, but "what the Christian repetition brings back, it

16. Oliver Davies, "Thinking Difference: A Comparative Study of Gilles Deleuze, Plotinus and Meister Eckhart," in *Deleuze and Religion*, ed. Mary Bryden (London: Routledge, 2001), 84.

brings back once, and only once: the wealth of Job and the child of Abraham, the resurrected body and the recovered self" (*LS*, 300–301). By contrast, eternal return frustrates any attempt at continuity or control over the future, any attempt to curb the crowned anarchies of difference and becoming. Because it frustrates all control and all hierarchical judgment, eternal return "is not a doctrine but the simulacrum of every doctrine (the highest irony); it is not a belief but the parody of every belief (the highest humor)" (*DR*, 95–96). Providence is replaced by chance, destiny by becoming, God by eternal return itself, transcendent order by immanent becoming.

The plane of immanence, the virtual, and eternal return are concepts by means of which Deleuze seeks to expel all traces of theological thinking from his philosophy. It would be a mistake, however, to think that Deleuze defines his account of eternal return, or indeed any other aspect of his thought, in explicit contradistinction to Christianity. In fact, he works hard to resist Christian theology's setting the agenda. Deleuze is very aware of the need for philosophy to escape theology's shadow, and one way for it to remain in that shadow is to retain the fundamental structure of the dogmatic image of thought while seeking to change particular concepts within that structure. This is what I have elsewhere called *imitative atheism*,[17] a purportedly atheistic thought continuing to work within structures given to it by theology.

Deleuze seeks to rid philosophy not only of God, but also of all the traces and echoes of God in the godlike structures of the unified human subject, the hierarchical state, and the idea of a unified and harmonious nature: "the death of God, the possibility of replacing God with humanity, all the God-Human

17. See Christopher Watkin, *Difficult Atheism: Post-Theological Thinking in Alain Badiou, Jean-Luc Nancy and Quentin Meillassoux* (Edinburgh: Edinburgh University Press, 2011).

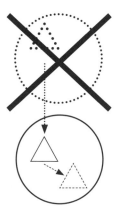

imitative atheism

Fig. 2.7. Imitative Atheism

permutations, etc. It's like Foucault said, we are no more human than God, the one dies with the other" (*DI*, 137).

In Deleuze's own terms, it is not quite right to say that he does not believe in God, as if God were a concept in relation to which one still had to take a position. Deleuze's aim is to set out a plane of immanence in which the very question of belief in God is no longer relevant, for the one who actively disbelieves in God "would still belong to the old plane as negative movement" (*WIP*, 74).

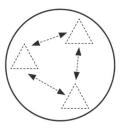

Deleuze's plane
of immanence

Fig. 2.8. The plane of immanence does not lack God. It is complete in itself.

The danger that Deleuze is seeking to avoid here is that immanence becomes negatively defined by transcendence, and that in vacating the space of transcendence it leaves that space unoccupied, ready for God to return. Deleuze wants not merely to reject belief in God, but to leave no place within his thought where God could be, to make the very idea of God unintelligible in the image of thought he sets forth. Getting rid of God in this way is not easily accomplished, however, and "it may be that believing in this world, in this life, becomes our most difficult task, or the task of a mode of existence still to be discovered on our plane of immanence today" (*WIP*, 75). The victory of atheism will be proclaimed when the death of God ceases to be a live question for philosophy: "For philosophers neither atheism nor the death of God are problems. . . . It is astonishing that philosophers still take the death of God to be tragic. Atheism is not a drama but the philosopher's serenity and philosophy's achievement" (*WIP*, 92, my translation).

3

IMPLICATIONS OF
DELEUZE'S PHILOSOPHY

I will conclude this survey of Deleuze's thought with three brief reflections dealing with specific aspects of his philosophy. First I will trace the implications of Deleuze's philosophy for the Cartesian subject and our understanding of the human body; next I examine the question of truth in Deleuze's thought and how his style of writing and the structure of his books reflect and embody his philosophical commitments; and in the final section I reflect on the ethics and politics that emerge in his writing.

The Subject and the Body

As I indicated at the end of the previous chapter, if Deleuze is to have done with God, then he must be rid of the concepts and ways of thinking that inherit from a theological framework. In fact, in a discussion of the philosopher Pierre Klossowski, Deleuze argues that God is the linchpin of a whole set of very familiar interrelated concepts:

> The order of God includes the following elements: the iden-
> tity of God as the ultimate foundation; the identity of the
> world as the ambient environment; the identity of the person
> as a well-founded agency; the identity of bodies as the base;
> and finally the identity of language as the power of denoting
> everything else. (*LS*, 292)

God, the world, the person, the body, and language stand or fall
together. In this section I will address how Deleuze rethinks the
identity of the person and the body in accord with his rejection
of the dogmatic image of thought.

The Western understanding of agency and personhood owes
much to Descartes' account of the subject, the concept of a unified,
self-conscious, rationally governed self epitomized in his *cogito ergo
sum*, "I am thinking, therefore I exist."[1] The subject is a concept
that fits with the dogmatic image of thought: all subjects are identical with each other as thinking things, and unchanging within
themselves insofar as they are self-conscious, rational beings:

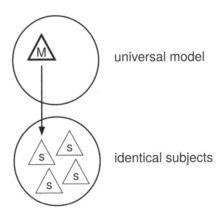

**Fig. 3.1. The dogmatic image of thought produces identical subjects
that conform to an ideal type.**

1. The subject is not the same as the human being. Babies, for example, are human
beings but have no concept of themselves as unified, rational selves.

The subject, then, is an instance of transcendence just like God (*LS*, 106); it is unchanging just like God, and it conforms to the judgment of God in being identical to other subjects. In short, "God survives as long as the I enjoys a subsistence, a simplicity and an identity which express the entirety of its resemblance to the divine" (*DR*, 86). Philosophers who thought they were overcoming God by replacing God with the human subject were gravely mistaken, Deleuze warns: they were merely substituting one transcendent theological concept for another (*DR*, 58). To sit humanity on God's throne is not to vanquish God but merely to give him a new name and exchange one deity, one ordering and organizing principle, for another. As for ducks, so for gods: if it organizes like a god, judges like a god, is unchanging like a god, and is self-identical like a god, then it is a god. Any claim to reverse Platonism and have done with God, therefore, must also dismantle the unified and self-identical *I*. Deleuze does this with his claim that the *I think* of Descartes is one effect among many of the interactions and arrangements of a swarm of "larval subjects" (*DR*, 78–79, 118–19) that never cohere into one stable, unified subject. In the same way that identities and essences are really products of flows of becoming that they mask and deny, so also the unified self is the product of a much more complex picture that it seeks to suppress:

> Underneath the self which acts are little selves which con-template and which render possible both the action and the active subject. We speak of our "self" only by virtue of these thousands of little witnesses which contemplate within us: it is always a third party who says "me." (*DR*, 75)

What we call the *self*, in the singular, is in fact a mask cover-ing over groups of pre-individual singularities or larval subjects. Whereas the fiction of the arborescent self subordinates all these little selves to the despotic control of the invented concept of the *self*, creating in the process a false interiority in its appeal to the "real me," the body without organs is understood as a series of larval subjects with no overarching organization, no significance taken in isolation, and no deep interiority behind or underneath the relations between them.

It is not only in the Cartesian subject that theology persists, however. Deleuze also sees the way we understand our bodies as a theological hangover, because he identifies the judgment of God with the organizing of the body as an organism, and organisms are theological. Deleuze is using the term *organism* with a specific sense: a hierarchical ordering of the body that "imposes upon it forms, functions, bonds, dominant and hier-archized organizations, organized transcendences" (*ATP*, 159). It is the bodily equivalent of Plato's distinction between Form and copy, with the primacy of identity over difference and being over becoming. This hierarchical way of ordering characteristic of the judgment of God is described by Deleuze and Guattari in *A Thousand Plateaus* as "arborescent." The image is of the branches, or the roots, of a tree: however many branches or roots there are, they are all connected to one central and organizing trunk, with a hierarchy of smaller and larger roots, thinner and thicker branches. Everything begins from, and is brought back to, this one center. This model of hierarchical, centralized organiza-tion is typical of the dogmatic image of thought, and is "the most classical and well reflected, oldest, and weariest kind of thought" (*ATP*, 5) in the Western tradition.

It is also the way in which the human self and body have traditionally been understood, with a single, rational center con-trolling all its faculties and all the organs of its body, disciplining them and setting them to work for efficient and productive ends. Differences are organized into neat, hierarchized oppositions and analogies (between the will and the appetite, for example), in

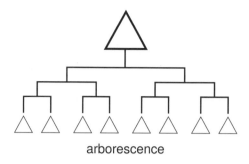

arborescence

Fig. 3.2. The Hierarchical Organization of Arborescence

what Deleuze calls an "arborification of multiplicities" (*ATP,* 506). It is also a model that, for Deleuze, has had its day: "We're tired of trees," he writes, and "we should stop believing in trees, roots, and radicals. They've made us suffer too much" (*ATP,* 15).

So if "one cannot conserve the self without also holding on to God" (*LS,* 294) and if "the death of God becomes effective only with the dissolution of the Self" (*DR,* 58), how does Deleuze dissolve the Self? Prior to the imposition of the unified, rational self by the dogmatic image of thought is what Deleuze calls the *body without organs* (BwO), and it is the BwO that he seeks to liberate from the judgment of God that constrains it to be an organism. The term *body without organs* is prone to misinterpretation. Deleuze does not have in mind a body without a liver, heart, brain, and so on; "the BwO is opposed not to the organs but to that organization of the organs called the organism" (*ATP,* 158). A body without organs is a body without the centralized, hierarchical organization that makes it into a unified, productive organism and makes it in the image of the judging God. We might think of it as a "nonhierarchical body" or a "body that is not centrally organized."

There are clear political stakes for Deleuze in the body without organs. The organization of bodies into centralized, unified, and hierarchical selves is a political move that favors a politics of the rational ordering of society and social control. In order to resist this political oppression of the body, the centralized self itself must be undone in order to reveal the "body without organs" that it has oppressed and exploited.

In addition to introducing the body without organs, Deleuze and Guattari take what we customarily think of as a self and its environment, flatten out the distinction between the two, and break them down into what they call *machines*. They use the term *machine* to describe this assemblage of parts because it places the focus on the interaction of individual elements rather than the overall purpose or integrity of the whole.

> Everywhere it is machines—real ones, not figurative ones: machines driving other machines, machines being driven by other machines, with all the necessary couplings and connections. An organ-machine is plugged into an energy-source-machine: the one produces a flow that the other interrupts. . . . Hence we are all handymen: each with his little machines. (*AO*, 1)

One of their famous examples of an assemblage of machines is a baby suckling at its mother's breast: a cupping machine (the mouth) connects with a milk-producing machine (the breast): "The breast is a machine that produces milk, and the mouth is a machine coupled to it" (*AO*, 1). It is the accumulation of these local connections, coupled together by flows of desire, that makes what we call a *self*. In the same way that difference precedes identity, these desiring-machines are operative before there is any sense of a *mother* or a *baby*: it is a desiring-machine that seeks the comfort of the breast, not an organism, just as it is from a swarm of larval subjects that the *I think* emerges, not from a unified subject.

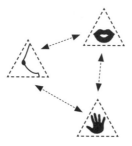

Fig. 3.3. The Machinic Body without Organs

As we saw in the discussion of Deleuze's flat ontology above, in speaking of desiring-machines he is seeking to break down the limits of the body, moving across elements that we would customarily divide between *self* and *other*, between the *body* and the *world*, and between *organic* and *inorganic*. A desiring-machine is any series of connections through which desire flows. Flows of desire can link a mouth to a breast, but also a hand to a tool, or a plant to the sun. In other words, there is no privilege of the human, and no strict dichotomy between *nature* and *culture*, for Deleuze's desiring-machines, as there would be for the traditional notion of the individual and its body.

In contrast to the arborescent hierarchy of the organism, Deleuze and Guattari characterize the machinic organization of the BwO as rhizomatic. A rhizome is a type of plant, a stem or root system that is not hierarchically organized and has no center or trunk, only nodes, roots, and shoots: "There are no points or positions in a rhizome, such as those found in a structure, tree, or root. There are only lines" (*ATP*, 8). Whereas trees always take a roughly similar shape, with a trunk connecting a root system to the branches and leaves, rhizomes have no determinate overall structure. In *A Thousand Plateaus*, Deleuze and Guattari give the example of couch grass, a rhizomatic grass that is the bane of gardeners for the way in which its rhizomes entangle themselves in the roots of trees and bushes. Its decentralized structure means that if any part of a rhizome of couch grass is left in the soil after attempted eradication, it can grow into a new plant.

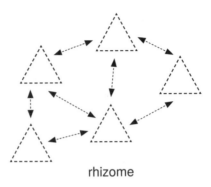

rhizome

Fig. 3.4. The Nonhierarchical Distribution of the Rhizome

The rhizome characterizes any noncentralized and nonhierarchized multiplicity, and stands in relation to the arborescent as Deleuze's overturning of Platonism does to Platonism itself:

> The tree is filiation, but the rhizome is alliance, uniquely alliance. The tree imposes the verb "to be," but the fabric of the rhizome is the conjunction, "and ... and ... and ..." This conjunction carries enough force to shake and uproot the verb "to be." (*ATP*, 25)

Deleuze and Guattari consider rhizomatic any nonhierarchical and noncentralized and proliferating series of connections, whether those connections are material in nature, organizations of power, or chains of meaning.

Truth and Style

We have already seen that, for Deleuze, the dogmatic image of thought is inextricably bound up with a particular set of political ideas, born out of Plato's political problem of distinguishing between the true philosopher and the false sophist, and with the aim of preserving the order and stability of the state. Plato creates in his ontology a perfect reflection of his politics: he gives himself the ontology that his politics requires. His philosophy, then, is guided and shaped not by a pure will to truth, but by pragmatic political ends.

Deleuze identifies this gambit of engineering an ontology to fit a preordained politics not only in Plato. Aristotle projects the ideal of the privileged adult male citizen onto the natural and onto the divine, and then justifies the privilege of the adult male citizen in terms of nature and the divine.[2] Kant is named by Deleuze as the quintessential philosopher of the state par excellence, who "turns the philosopher into the judge" (*WIP*, 72) to mirror the function of the state judiciary. Kant derives his idea of the transcendental, judging subject from the legislative state, and then justifies the state in terms of the subject. His philosophy is a reflection of the juridical system that his philosophy supports, "tracing its doctrine of faculties onto the organs of state power" (*ATP*, 376). Following a similar pattern, Deleuze and Guattari see monotheism as lending itself to despotic, imperialist states (*WIP*, 43).

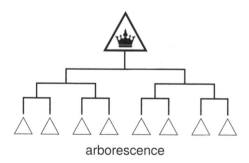

arborescence

Fig. 3.5. The Arborescent Organization of the Imperialist State

2. This point is made by John Protevi in "The Organism and the Judgment of God," in *Deleuze and Religion*, ed. Mary Bryden (London: Routledge, 2001), 31.

How Does Deleuze Know That His View Is True?

This, for Deleuze and Guattari, is the pattern of all philosophical systems: not a disinterested search for truth but a complicity of ontology and politics all the way down. They see their own position as no different: they give themselves an ontology that will facilitate their ethical and political aims. It is worth pausing a moment, before we press on to discuss Deleuze and Guattari's ethics and politics, to reflect on a question that will have been raised, I suspect, in the minds of many readers of this book: "how does Deleuze know that what he is saying is true?" It is a question that exercises theologian John Milbank in *Theology and Social Theory*. "If Being remains in itself unknowable, always absent and concealed," asks Milbank, "then how do we justify the characterization of Being as univocity?"[3] We cannot, he concludes, pointing to what he sees as "the element of sheer preference" in Deleuze's fundamental ontology.[4] These questions are easy to pose, but not quite as easy to answer as Milbank assumes, unless we betray Deleuze, the question, or both. I propose to make eight observations with the intention of showing why this question prevents us from understanding what Deleuze is trying to do.

The first observation to make is that the question "is it true?" belongs in the dogmatic image of thought. It is the question par excellence to distinguish between the icon and the simulacrum, and we have already seen how Deleuze suspects such a question of political motivations. It is out of an addiction to the dogmatic image of thought that one privileges what Deleuze, after Nietzsche, calls the *will to truth* (see, for example, *NaP*, 94–96).

Second, by Deleuze's lights, asking of any philosophical system "is it true?" is problematic, because each system brings its own criteria for what counts as a valid answer to that question.

---

3. John Milbank, *Theology and Social Theory* (Oxford: Blackwell, 2008), 306.
4. Milbank, *Theology and Social Theory*, 308.

Judged empirically, empiricism seems the "truest" of all systems. In terms of its power of a priori reasoning, idealism looks the "truest." The criteria of truth are part of the system, not something outside all systems by which they can each be impartially judged. In *Difference and Repetition* (187), Deleuze expresses this in terms of conic sections. Imagine taking a cone, standing it on its base, and slicing it in two with a knife at an angle of forty-five degrees. Now throw away the top half of the cone. The forty-five-degree surface of the cone base is a conic section. Slicing at different angles and heights will yield different conic sections. Each conic section is complete in itself, yet not the whole story of the cone, just as each philosophical system is self-consistent and yet not an exhaustive account of the world.[5]

The third reason why the question of truth is problematic for Deleuze is that it turns us away from the world, to abstract and unchanging concepts that betray the flux and becoming of reality. Whatever we might try to say about the world will always fall short of its complex becoming.

Fourth, Deleuze's interest in the question of truth is not primarily in answering it, but in questioning what motivates it. Deleuze follows Nietzsche in interrogating the reason why we pursue the "will to truth": whose interests does it serve? Who stands to gain from enforcing a strict definition of *truth*? Do those interests suppress becoming and difference, or encourage them?

Fifth, asking of any philosophy whether it is true misunderstands what philosophy itself is. Deleuze and Guattari reply to the eponymous question of *What Is Philosophy?* with a straight and succinct answer: philosophy is "the discipline that involves *creating* concepts" (*WIP*, 5)—in other words, creating ideas that help us to see and live in the world in new ways, such as Plato's

5. Henry Somers-Hall, "Introduction," in *The Cambridge Companion to Deleuze*, ed. Daniel W. Smith and Henry Somers-Hall (Cambridge: Cambridge University Press, 2012), 7.

creation of the Forms (*WIP*, 6) or Kant's transcendental, legislating subject. Note that philosophy creates concepts for Deleuze, rather than discovering them. To discover ready-made concepts in the world would be the modus operandi of the representation and recognition at the heart of the dogmatic image of thought, but in a philosophy of immanent becoming, the imperative is to be inventive and to proliferate difference. It is also important to recognize that, for Deleuze, concepts are always responses to problems (such as the problem of distinguishing the sophist from the philosopher in Plato), not foundations in their own right. So the question to ask of a concept is not "is it true?" but "to what problem is it a response?," and the criterion by which such concepts are to be judged is not whether they are true, but what they allow us to see and how they allow us to act.

Sixth, the criterion of truth is replaced in Deleuze's thinking by two other measures: interest and usefulness. Let us take interest first: "Philosophy does not consist in knowing and is not inspired by truth. Rather, it is categories like Interesting, Remarkable, or Important that determine success or failure" (*WIP*, 82). As for usefulness, in the course of a conversation with Michel Foucault, Deleuze insists that "a theory is exactly like a box of tools. . . . It must be useful. It must function."[6] The toolbox metaphor is an instructive one. We do not mount our tools on the walls of our houses to gaze at them admiringly, nor do we simply write books that describe our tools in loving detail. Tools are to be used on particular, local projects; they prove themselves when they help us to get a job done. Similarly, theories are not there to admire or wax lyrical about, but to perform certain, specific, and local tasks in the world, after which they can be laid aside and other tools chosen to address other projects and tasks.

---

6. Gilles Deleuze and Michel Foucault, "Intellectuals and Power," in *Language, Counter-Memory, Practice: Selected Essays and Interviews by Michel Foucault*, ed. Donald F. Bouchard (Ithaca, NY: Cornell University Press, 1977), 208.

Interest and usefulness are not as unusual criteria as may at first appear. Why has Plato's philosophy had such an enduring hold on the Western imagination? Because it is true? No one has been able to show conclusively that it is. But it has certainly drawn the interest of generations of philosophers, and generated libraries of commentary and critique. And it has certainly proved itself useful in providing explanations of everything from language to the origin of our knowledge and the possibility of grouping individual things in the world in meaningful categories. Philosophers do not know whether Plato's system is true, but they have found it exceedingly interesting and useful.

Seventh, concepts are interesting and useful for Deleuze in direct proportion to their promotion of the dynamic becoming of life itself: "There are never any criteria other than the tenor of existence, the intensification of life" (*WIP*, 74). The litmus test is not whether a philosophical concept corresponds to some pregiven reality, but the style of life to which it leads: does it intensify the becoming and difference of life, or stifle it? For the dogmatic image of thought, thinking is about recognizing and representing reality; for Deleuze and Nietzsche, thinking is about "discovering, inventing, new possibilities of life" (*NaP*, 101). In fact, this concern trumps the question of truthfulness, such that Nietzsche can famously write of the God of divine providence that he "is so absurd that we would have to get rid of him even if he *did* exist."[7]

Eighth and finally, Deleuze displaces the question of truth and falsity away from propositions (this is a true image; that is a false simulacrum) and makes them qualify the problems that condition them (the problem of the "true image" is a false problem). We have the (empirical) truths we deserve as a function of

---

7. Aaron Ridley and Judith Norman, eds., *Nietzsche: The Anti-Christ, Ecce Homo, Twilight of the Idols: And Other Writings* (Cambridge: Cambridge University Press, 2005), 52 (§ 53).

the problems that we have been able to pose, and the means and terms we create for posing them.

Style

It must go down as one of the most tongue-in-cheek litotes[8] in all the secondary literature when Philip Goodchild comments that Deleuze is "not a light read."[9] Indeed, Deleuze's forbidding style has scared off many an intrepid reader, and frustrated many more. Deleuze is, without a doubt, philosophically forbidding, yet he has very little of the wordplay and homophony[10] that characterize most of Derrida's writing. Deleuze's books are hard to read because his philosophical ideas are complex, and the concepts that he invents are precise and counterintuitive. For those with patterns of understanding and expectations of reading shaped to some extent by the dogmatic image of thought—which is almost certainly every Western reader of this book—reading Deleuze is hard work.

Part of the reason that reading Deleuze is such a slog is that his overturning of the dogmatic image of thought demands a new style of writing and a different understanding of what a book should be. Once more, the prevailing notions of what it means to write well and what a book is are deeply shaped by the dogmatic image of thought, without most of us ever reflecting on that influence. Think, for example, of the subject-predicate style of most discursive prose: "x is y," "this is that," "this animal in front of me is a dog." Subject-predicate propositions assume that there are ready-made facts out there in the world waiting to be discovered and assigned to unchanging categories, and it assumes that our language can stand apart from the reality it describes, explaining

8. Understated verbal irony that uses a negative to express a positive.

9. Philip Goodchild, *Deleuze and Guattari: An Introduction to the Politics of Desire* (London: Sage, 1996), 1.

10. Words pronounced alike but different in meaning.

it with cool detachment. In short, it is a way of writing perfectly attuned to the premium on recognition and representation in the dogmatic image of thought, but spectacularly inept at expressing creative becoming.

To argue Deleuze's corner, a little reflection will show us that this understanding of language is naive. Language does not sit outside reality at all, but contributes to shaping our perception of the world. Changing the language we use contributes to changing our understanding of a situation. If this is not the case, why has there been such a discussion of gender-neutral pronouns in recent critical thought, and why, for example, is the abortion debate characterized by the clash of two contrasting vocabularies to describe the same events? Language is not a detached and neutral medium through which reality is unproblematically given to us, and the language and style we use when we write and speak cannot be divorced from the positions we hold.

Language and style, then, cannot be neutral. "Great philosophers are also great stylists" (*Ne*, 164), Deleuze insists. We see this in the way in which philosophical writing can pull and prod at syntax, which is "a sort of straining toward something that isn't syntactic, nor even linguistic (something outside language)" (*Ne*, 164). Syntax itself is a reflection of an image of thought, and so for Deleuze "there are no straight lines, neither in things nor in language. Syntax is the set of necessary detours that are created in each case to reveal the life in things" (*ECC*, 2).

We also see the outworking of Deleuze's image of thought in his changing vocabulary. Each new major text introduces a new set of concepts, and terms that are of central importance in Deleuze's thought in his earlier writing (*reversal of Platonism*, for example, or *univocity* or *simulacrum*) disappear in later texts. How could it be otherwise, if concepts are tools that are useful for completing local tasks for a period of time, rather than timeless Platonic Forms? Deleuze's vocabulary embodies the difference and becoming that his philosophy evokes.

In line with his rejection of the dogmatic image of thought and his own philosophical commitments, Deleuze writes not to represent the world accurately but to change it and to create new trajectories of becoming. He develops this stylistic trait over time. His earlier texts, such as *Difference and Repetition*, retain a recognizably linear structure, unfolding an argument one chapter after another, but in the later works coauthored with Félix Guattari, the structure of the text is not arborescent but rhizomatic. The most developed example of this style is *A Thousand Plateaus*, which Deleuze and Guattari describe as "a little machine" and a "body without organs" (*ATP*, 4). The text is structured as fifteen numbered sections, ranging from thirteen to seventy-eight pages in length in the English translation, which can be read in any order and between any two or more of which connections can be drawn. The plateaus are not hierarchically organized, nor are they framed in terms of a beginning, middle, and end.[11]

In order to distinguish this way of writing from the style characteristic of the dogmatic image of thought, Deleuze and Guattari insist on the distinction between the arborescent *root-book* and the *rhizome-book*.[12] A root-book is a form of writing that seeks to present a faithful image of the world (*ATP*, 5). It sends down one main taproot and organizes all its material around that center, which Deleuze equates with the book's single vertical spine (*ATP*, 5). It is a form that is incapable of reaching an understanding of multiplicity. A rhizome-book, by contrast, does not stand over against the world as its faithful reflection, but "forms

11. *The Logic of Sense* is also composed of "series" rather than chapters, which one can supposedly read in any order.

12. Deleuze introduces a third model of the book, the *radicle-system*, or fascicular root, which, though it gives the appearance of decentralized multiplicity, still sends out secondary roots from a single principal taproot.

a rhizome with the world" such that "there is a parallel evolution of the book and the world" (*ATP*, 11). The rhizome-book is not separate from the world in which it exists, but participates in the same flows of desire and the same machinic assemblages as everything else. Nor is the author considered to be transcendent with respect to the book. The three realities of author, book, and world that form the transcendent structure of the root-book are systematically transgressed in the rhizome-book:

> There is no longer a tripartite division between a field of reality (the world) and a field of representation (the book) and a field of subjectivity (the author). Rather, an assemblage establishes connections between certain multiplicities drawn from each of these orders, so that a book has no sequel nor the world as its object nor one or several authors as its subject. (*ATP*, 23)

Once more, Deleuze's flat ontology demands that we rethink in a radical way what we understand a book to be. Finally, like the rhizome itself, the rhizome-book has no beginning, middle, or end. This transforms the book both for the author and for the reader: "It's not easy to see things in the middle, rather than looking down on them from above or up at them from below, or from left to right or right to left: try it, you'll see that everything changes" (*ATP*, 23).

Ethics and Politics

The profound differences we have remarked between the relative status of truth and the differences in style between the dogmatic image of thought and in Deleuze's philosophy already begin to sketch for us the distinctive contours of Deleuze's ethics and politics. Once more we find that it is a case of the contrast between the vertical and the horizontal, the arborescent and the rhizomatic, identity and becoming. Let us first consider the question of ethics. In broad terms, whereas the dogmatic image of thought establishes a code of true and false, right and wrong, good and evil, Deleuze's ethical thought can be understood in terms of three elements: life, creativity, and maximizing potential.

Deleuze's highest good—though of course this good is not "high" in the sense of transcendent but in the sense of preeminent—is life, and his ethics can be understood not as a moral code but as "a matter . . . of evaluating every being, every action and passion, even every value, in relation to the life which they involve" (C2, 141). In the absence of any transcendent yardstick against which to measure life, it is life itself that becomes the ethical measure. The affirmation of life is not quite as straightforward as it might sound, however. We must not presume that by "life" Deleuze means only human life, an anthropocentrism that he is at pains to avoid. The preservation of human life is "good" only from a restricted, human point of view. In the same way as the simulacrum is inferior only once we have taken the contingent decision to privilege the "true" copy, so also nonhuman life is valued less than the human only following a rather strategic and self-interested decision to make it so.[13] Evil is always evil *for someone*, and from some particular perspective.

What is it about life that is positively coded for Deleuze? The answer is to be found in the way he draws on Spinoza's notion of *conatus*, the effort to persevere in being. For Deleuze as for Spinoza, this effort is one of maximizing one's potential and power to act, maximizing one's essence, which—as we have already seen—is for Deleuze a power to become and change.

13. This point is made by Claire Colebrook, *Understanding Deleuze* (Sydney: Allen and Unwin, 2003), 161.

Ethics has become indistinguishable from ontology: our essence is that, in becoming and differentiating, we maximize our potential; similarly, our ethical imperative is to maximize our potential. This gives Deleuze an immanent notion of the good: "the good is when a body directly compounds its relation with ours, and, with all or part of its power, increases ours" (*SPP*, 22).

In a more Nietzschean register, this embrace of life is expressed in terms of affirmation. In contrast to a Christianity in which he sees only untrammeled renunciation of this life, Deleuze echoes Nietzsche's ethics of affirmation, welcoming and embracing what happens, not as a passive acceptance of whatever comes along but as a free creation of one's own life:

> To affirm is not to take responsibility for, to take on the burden of what is, but to release, to set free what lives. To affirm is to unburden: not to load life with the weight of higher values, but to create new values which are those of life, which make life light and active. (*NaP*, 185)

This affirmative self-creation is a way to walk in step with the essence of things as an abundance of becoming and difference—as Deleuze puts it, "to become worthy of what happens to us, . . . to become the offspring of one's own events" (*LS*, 149).

It is of first importance for Deleuze that this creative affirmation be autonomous. It is the arborescent hierarchy of the dogmatic image of thought that imposes conformity to an image that originates outside the individual. For Deleuze, by stark contrast, the value of autonomy rivals even that of life itself: "Better death than the health which we are given" (*LS*, 160). If we do not invent and proliferate our own concepts, then our thinking and actions will be governed by someone else's concepts, complete with their own political agenda, such as Plato's concepts of the Form, copy, and simulacrum.

We will do well to pause a moment in order to feel the force of Deleuze's argument here. Dear reader, do you want someone else to do your thinking for you? If, every time you had an important decision to make, you called a particular telephone number and the person on the end of the line, whom you had never met and whom you did not know, told you what to do in a way that you were obliged to follow, you would not (let me hazard a guess) be completely happy with the situation. That, for Deleuze, is what it is like to live in the dogmatic image of thought: letting that image tell you what reality is all about and how you should act within it, without even realizing that this is what it is doing. In the introduction to *The Deleuze Dictionary*, Claire Colebrook frames this resistance to heteronomy in terms of a self-consciously ironic categorical imperative: "Live in such a way that one's life diverges from any given principle."[14]

In addition to this ethics of life and affirmation, Deleuze and Guattari's politics also both informs and draws on their ontological commitments. In the place of the hierarchical, authoritarian state associated with a Platonic or Kantian ontology, their politics reflects their understanding of ontology as rhizomatic. They begin not with the individual, unified subject as the political unit, but with a noncentralized, nonhierarchical proliferation of becoming and flows of desire.

If transcendence and arborescent thought are hierarchical and aristocratic, then Deleuze's rhizomatic insistence on immanence and the univocity of being is egalitarian:

> Against Descartes, Spinoza posits the equality of all forms of being, and the univocity of reality which follows from this equality. The philosophy of immanence appears from all

---

14. Claire Colebrook, "Introduction," in *The Deleuze Dictionary: Revised Edition*, ed. Adrian Parr (Edinburgh: Edinburgh University Press, 2010), 5.

viewpoints as the theory of unitary Being, equal Being, common and univocal Being. (*EPS*, 167)

To hold to the univocity of being is to affirm all being equally, and to deny any hierarchy of beings. This egalitarian impulse shows itself in two of Deleuze and Guattari's prominent political themes: their politics is nomadic and minoritarian.

Deleuze and Guattari develop the concept of nomadism in *A Thousand Plateaus* not to designate itinerant communities in search of grazing for their livestock, but to designate any group whose principle of organization is within itself, not imposed from above. Deleuze offers a pastoral example to clarify what he means. *Nomad*, he notes, is from the Greek *nomos*, usually taken to mean "law," but *nomos* itself derives from the root *nemo*, which means to pasture livestock by "scattering" (*ATP*, 557n51) them across the countryside as opposed to arranging them neatly. A collection of grazing animals is not structured according to a principle imposed on them from the outside; they are free each to find their own corner of pasture on which to ruminate. This lack of imposed structure is contrasted to the order of *logos*, which Deleuze identifies with the transcendence of the ordering idea and the judgment of God. It is the city that is ruled by laws, whereas by contrast the grazing land on its outskirts is the scattered *nomos*. A nomadic politics, then, is a politics that does not impose rigid order from above but allows fluid arborescent relations to emerge from below.

Second, in *A Thousand Plateaus* Deleuze and Guattari elaborate what they call a *minoritarian* politics. When we hear *majoritarian* and *minoritarian* in this context, we should not think that they mean the same as *majority* and *minority*. Majoritarian and minoritarian do not equate with big and small, but with norm-setting and norm-transgressing. In Deleuze and Guattari's language, the majoritarian is that which provides the yardstick, the constant against which everything else is measured:

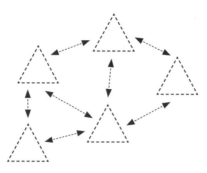

Fig. 3.6. The Fluid and Spontaneous Order of Nomadic Politics

> Let us suppose that the constant or standard is the average adult white-heterosexual European-male speaking a standard language . . . . It is obvious that "man" holds the majority, even if he is less numerous than mosquitoes, children, women, blacks, peasants, homosexuals, etc. That is because he appears twice, once in the constant and again in the variable from which the constant is extracted. Majority assumes a state of power and domination, not the other way around. (*ATP*, 105)

A majoritarian politics would start with such a constant—say the middle-aged affluent white heterosexual Christian male—and build a system to suit that constant, which is then simply understood as *man* or *humanity*. It would then invite other groups to join the system; women and other minorities are granted access only to the extent that they acquiesce to play by the rules of the majoritarian faction. Like an eternal Platonic Form, the constant remains unchanging regardless of who is included in it. If there is a rhetoric of equality, it is a veil for saying that everyone is equal to the extent that they conform to the constant.

It should be clear from this description that simply including minorities in the majority is still a majoritarian position. Extending an olive branch to minority groups with the implied message "you, too, can be a white man" is more imperialistic than magnanimous. A true minoritarian politics, by contrast, revels in difference and becoming, and therefore "it is important not to confuse 'minoritarian,' as a becoming or process, with a 'minority,' as an aggregate or a state" (*ATP*, 291). A minoritarian group has no fixed identity but is a process of becoming. Deleuze and Guattari explore a series of such becomings in *A Thousand Plateaus*, including becoming-woman, becoming-animal, becoming-imperceptible, and becoming-minor. Becoming-woman, they argue, is the gatekeeper of all minoritarian becoming, not because there are fewer women than men, but because there is no fixed standard in the Western tradition for what a woman should be. Becoming-woman is a constant troubling or variation of the static male constant, cutting across its boundaries and destabilizing it.

When they insist on the importance of becoming-woman, therefore, Deleuze and Guattari are not seeking to champion the female against the male. Their becoming-woman is not in symmetrical opposition to being man, nor does the term imply that woman is the destination and final resting place of becoming. Their attack is deeper than that: they want to use the nonspecific, fluid category *woman* to dismantle the categories of *woman* and *man* insofar as they are both used to designate fixed identities. This is why, in *A Thousand Plateaus*, Deleuze and Guattari insist on becoming-woman as a trajectory toward not a uniform femininity, but "a thousand tiny sexes" (*ATP*, 213) liberated from their incarceration in the restrictive binary categories of *male* and *female*, in the same way that Platonic identities for Deleuze fix and atrophy becoming. Whatever appears fixed is so only because of its suppression of difference.

This constant disruption of fixed identity itself has political importance for Deleuze, because without the stable, responsible individual, the mechanisms of repression and control characteristic of the dogmatic image of thought cannot continue to function:

You see, the forces of repression always need a Self that can be assigned, they need determinate individuals on which to exercise their power. When we become the least bit fluid, when we slip away from the assignable Self, when there is no longer any person on whom God can exercise his power or by whom He can be replaced, the police lose it. (*DI*, 138)

This is no abstract theory for Deleuze. The student protests of May 1968 demonstrate such a refusal of the norms on which the repressive state relies in order to exert its control. These protests, coming in the year of the publication of Deleuze's breakthrough text *Difference and Repetition*, encapsulate much of what is important in Deleuzian politics. They were nomadic, forming spontaneous groups of students rather than being ordered from above by the trade unions or the Communist Party, and they were minoritarian, seeking to disrupt the fixed categories of university and social life.

INTERLUDE

DELEUZE AND THE THEOLOGIANS

I would now like to bring Deleuze's thought into conversation with the Bible. My approach will borrow on occasion from existing attempts to stage a debate between Deleuze and theology (see the bibliography at the end of this volume for more details). Principally, I am attempting neither a Deleuzian reading of Christianity nor a Christian baptism of Deleuze. Such exercises remind me of the classic BBC Radio 4 comedy quiz show *I'm Sorry I Haven't a Clue*, on which one task given to the panel of comedians was to sing the words of one song to the tune of another. The results were often hilarious, but rarely musically satisfying. My approach in what follows, then, is neither "Deleuze to the tune of the Bible" nor "the Bible to the tune of Deleuze"; my aim is to let both parties play their own melody in their own way, and only then to find harmonies and dissonances between them. The approach I intend to take has two main features: it seeks to engage the whole of Deleuze's thought with the whole of the Bible, and it seeks to draw Deleuze and the Bible into conversation in the first instance around the problems they address.

The Whole of Deleuze's Thought;
the Whole of the Bible

Part of what it means to adhere to the principle of *audi alteram partem*[1] when seeking to engage a conversation between the Bible and a particular philosopher is that the nature and parameters of that conversation should be rethought with each fresh engagement, in a way that respects the specificities of the two parties involved. In Deleuze's case, one of the main features of his thought to be kept in mind in this respect is that it should be approached as a system of mutually informing concepts rather than a pick-and-mix bag of isolable ideas that can be extracted and studied one by one.

It is out of respect for this holistic principle that I have approached Deleuze through the notion of the *image of thought* in the first part of this book: seen as an element of a particular image of thought, each concept finds its meaning in terms of its relation to the other concepts in the same image. Claire Colebrook, one of the most astute writers on Deleuze, rightly stresses this point: "No term in [Deleuze's] work is capable of being defined in itself; any single term makes sense only in its relation to the whole which it helps to create."[2] It is therefore too quick to ask questions such as "what fills the space left by

1. *Audi alteram partem* (Latin: "listen to the other side") is one of the main principles governing the engagement between the Bible and secular philosophy in my work. It holds that a Christian engagement with a secular philosopher should begin by seeking to understand the philosopher in a way that those who know her or him best will recognize as faithful, including an understanding of why the moves made by the philosopher are not only warranted but good and attractive in their eyes. See Christopher Watkin, *Jacques Derrida*, Great Thinkers (Phillipsburg, NJ: P&R Publishing, 2017), xxv–xxvi; *Michel Foucault*, Great Thinkers (Phillipsburg, NJ: P&R Publishing, 2018), 78–79.

2. Claire Colebrook, *Gilles Deleuze*, Routledge Critical Thinkers (London: Routledge, 2001), 4. See also Claire Colebrook, *Understanding Deleuze* (Sydney: Allen and Unwin, 2003), xix.

God in Deleuze's thought?" or to compare a concept abstracted from Deleuze (such as the virtual) to a concept abstracted from the biblical canon. Our task is to bring into conversation two images of thought, not two concepts within the same image of thought.

In the Derrida volume in this Great Thinkers series, I judged that the best way to engage the range of Derrida's thought was to focus on the prologue to John's Gospel. A similarly localized approach was chosen in the volume on Michel Foucault, focusing on the motif of the "great reversal" in Philippians 2 and 1 Corinthians 1. In view of the importance of the image of thought for Deleuze, by contrast, I do not think that such a passage-based approach to the Bible will serve our purposes well at all. We need an approach that, *per impossibile*, brings the whole of the Bible and the understanding of the world that emerges from it to bear on the whole of Deleuze's thought, or at least an approach that seeks to approach the Bible as we approach Deleuze, realizing that every biblical idea requires the context of the whole biblical revelation in order to be adequately understood.

In order to come as close as we can to such an approach in a book of this size, I have chosen to stage a series of encounters between Deleuze and the Bible that follow the salvation-historical schema of creation, fall, redemption, and consummation. In other words, I take not a systematic but a biblical theological approach, following the work pioneered by Geerhardus Vos in his 1948 *Biblical Theology*.[3] The contention underpinning Vos's endeavor—namely, that the biblical canon tells a coherent story moving from creation to new creation—is given expression in Christian philosophical discourse under a number of different labels. Kevin Vanhoozer and John Milbank both insist on the importance of

---

3. Geerhardus Vos, *Biblical Theology: Old and New Testaments* (Eugene, OR: Wipf and Stock, 1975).

the Christian mythos[4] or story, and Vanhoozer evokes what he calls the "mythopoetic framework of Scripture,"[5] claiming that it is a "comprehensive (and canonical) interpretative framework that should govern Christian thinking about everything."[6] We can represent the biblical mythos very schematically in terms of a graph the horizontal axis of which represents time, and the vertical axis the extent to which God's kingdom is fulfilled.[7]

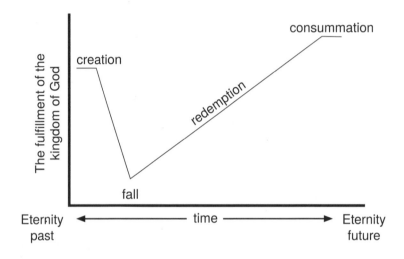

Fig. I.1. The Emplotted Biblical Mythos of Creation, Fall, Redemption, and Consummation

4. *Mythos* (or transliterated *muthos*) is Greek for "plot." It is the word that Aristotle uses when describing tragic emplotment in his *Poetics*, and is dealt with at length in Paul Ricœur, *Time and Narrative, Volume 1*, trans. Kathleen McLaughlin and David Pellauer (Chicago: University of Chicago Press, 1990).

5. Kevin Vanhoozer, "Pilgrim's Digress: Christian Thinking on and about the Post/modern Way," in *Christianity and the Postmodern Turn: Six Views*, ed. Myron B. Penner (Grand Rapids: Baker, 2005), 85.

6. Vanhoozer, "Pilgrim's Digress," 85.

7. This focus on the kingdom draws on Graeme Goldsworthy's *Gospel and Kingdom* (Milton Keynes, UK: Paternoster, 2012), and simplifies the graphical presentation of Goldsworthy's schema in Vaughan Roberts, *God's Big Picture: Tracing the Storyline of the Bible* (Leicester: Inter-Varsity Press, 2012).

Creation, fall, redemption, and consummation are, of course, only indicative placeholders for a mythos more rich and complex than these four key turning points alone. As Donald A. Carson stresses in his *Christ and Culture Revisited*:

> That stance is most likely to be deeply Christian which attempts to integrate all the major biblically determinate turning points in the history of redemption: creation, fall, the call of Abraham, the exodus and the giving of the law, the rise of the monarchy and the rise of the prophets, the exile, the incarnation, the ministry and death and resurrection of Jesus Christ, the onset of the kingdom of God, the coming of the spirit and the consequent ongoing eschatological tension between the "already" and the "not yet," the return of Christ and the prospect of a new heaven and a new earth.[8]

The fourfold schema is nevertheless helpful as a shorthand for this more verbose articulation. One feature of adopting a biblical theological approach is that it brings the motif of time into the center of our consideration. It will be important in the discussion that follows to contrast Deleuze's and the Bible's accounts of temporality, not least because doing so itself reveals a series of both resonances and dissonances between the two. Deleuze has his own understanding of time (Nietzschean eternal return, Bergsonian duration), and we must also let the Bible unfold its own distinctive temporalities.[9]

8. Donald A. Carson, *Christ and Culture Revisited* (Grand Rapids: Eerdmans, 2008), 81.

9. The plural *temporalities* is important here. The creation-fall-redemption-consummation schema should not lead us to assume, for example, that biblical time is straightforwardly "linear" as opposed to a supposedly "cyclical" Greek time. For an indication of the complexity of the notion of time in different genres of biblical writing, see Paul Ricœur, "Biblical Time," in *Figuring the Sacred: Religion, Narrative and Imagination*, ed. Mark I. Wallace, trans. David Pellauer (Minneapolis: Fortress

One further happy consequence of this approach is that it will allow the Bible to present its own ideas in its own way, in order to produce a philosophical account that is, in Alvin Plantinga's words, "less accommodation to current fashion and more Christian self-confidence."[10] Finally, adopting a biblical theological model of engagement also introduces and demonstrates another possible approach (in addition to those of the Derrida and Foucault volumes) to bringing philosophers into conversation with the Bible. What is lost in the approach of this present volume is a developed engagement with a particular biblical passage or passages. What is gained is a much more comprehensive account of the Christian story and biblical truth to bring to bear on Deleuze's thought.

A Problem-Based Approach

As well as taking a biblical theological approach to Deleuze, I propose to begin not with what Deleuze and the Bible say, but with the problems or questions to which they respond. This is an approach commended by Deleuze himself in a different context: "An organism is nothing if not the solution to a problem, as are each of its differenciated organs, such as the eye which solves a light 'problem'" (*DR*, 211). As Philip Goodchild notes, "the sense and function of Deleuze and Guattari's thought only emerges when considered in relation to the problems and processes that are at work in it."[11] Indeed, Deleuze seeks to rehabilitate the value of the clear articulation of a problem in the context of an intellectual culture obsessed with solutions: "Already in mathematics,

---

Press, 1995), 167–80.

10. From "Advice to Christian Philosophers," inaugural lecture to the John A. O'Brien Chair of Philosophy at the University of Notre Dame on November 4, 1983.

11. Philip Goodchild, *Deleuze and Guattari: An Introduction to the Politics of Desire* (London: Sage, 1996), vii.

and still more in metaphysics, the effort of invention consists most often in raising the problem, in creating the terms in which it will be stated" (*B*, 15). The dogmatic image of thought comes into focus when it is understood in terms of the problem of how to tell true from false copies, and Deleuze's own thought makes sense in terms of the problem of whether, and how, philosophy can understand change and transformation.

This problem-based approach avoids the elaborate and sterile "spot the difference" exercise that could issue from seeking to compare Deleuze and the Bible, in favor of asking how the Bible responds to, or rethinks, the problems from which Deleuze's philosophy begins. In each of the sections that follow, I will begin with a problem that Deleuze seeks to address, taken from the first part of this book. This does mean that, to some extent, the conversation is being conducted on Deleuze's territory, though there is enough overlap in the problems they address to be able to let both Deleuze and the Bible speak in their own voice. Finally, a problem-based approach will allow us to see Deleuze and the Bible not only at loggerheads, but also shoulder to shoulder in addressing common concerns. Perhaps most tellingly, we will see that Deleuze and Plato often share assumptions or positions in common that the Bible diagonalizes.[12]

---

12. Diagonalization describes the way in which the Bible frequently frustrates the categories of secular culture, that "it falls into neither of the categories on offer, but does not utterly reject them, either, while showing them both to be inadequate." Watkin, *Jacques Derrida*, 82. "To diagonalize a choice in this way is to refuse the two (or more) alternatives it offers and elaborate a position that is neither reducible nor utterly unrelated to them." Christopher Watkin, *Thinking through Creation: Genesis 1 and 2 as Tools of Cultural Critique* (Phillipsburg, NJ: P&R Publishing, 2017), 28.

PART 2

READING DELEUZE
READING THEOLOGY

4

TRINITY AND DIFFERENCE

One of the main problems to which both the dogmatic image of thought and Deleuze's philosophy respond is how to account for the one, the many, and the relationship between them. It is also a central concern of Christian theology. In Deleuze's case, we have seen that it is not as simple as saying that he privileges the many over the one. The formula "PLURALISM = MONISM" (*ATP*, 20) captures better than any simple opposition the way in which Deleuze's thought stresses both the univocity of being (in his later works: the *plane of immanence*) and radical difference. Similarly, the orthodox Christian doctrine of the Trinity has resisted privileging the one over the many or vice versa, as John Milbank rightly points out.[1] Despite this similarity in approach, however, there are marked differences.

Deleuze's own understanding of Christianity is rather free of complexity in this regard: "the Christian simplificatio" (*LS*,

---

1. See the discussion of equal ultimacy in Christopher Watkin, *Jacques Derrida*, Great Thinkers (Phillipsburg, NJ: P&R Publishing, 2017), 86–90; John Milbank, *Theology and Social Theory* (Oxford: Blackwell, 2008), 381.

297) is the reduction of the many to the one. Deleuze is perhaps thinking of the Plotinian emanation of existence from
unity here, but his characterization seems to have little in common with orthodox Trinitarianism. The distinctiveness of the
Christian Trinitarian approach is not that there is no dichotomy
of the one and the many, but, as Milbank rightly points out, that
the many and the one are related peacefully.[2] Hart goes as far
as to say—and I think the proposition warranted—that there is
no fundamental distinction between the one and the many in
Christianity: "the truly unexpected implication of Trinitarian
dogma is that Christian thought has no metaphysics of the
one and the many, the same and the different, because that is a
polarity that has no place in the Christian narrative."[3]

Seen from this point of view, Deleuze and Plato share the
same understanding of the difference between being and becoming, diverging only in which of the two terms they choose to
privilege. Hart expresses this proximity between Deleuze's
Heraclitean emphasis on difference and Plato's Parmenidean
privilege of unity and order with characteristic poetic flair:

> There is a specular infinity in mutually defining opposites:
> Parmenides and Heracleitos gaze into one another's eyes, and
> the story of being springs up between them; just as two mir-
> rors set before one another prolate their depths indefinitely,
> repeating an opposition that recedes forever along an illusory
> corridor without end, seeming to span all horizons and con-
> tain all things, the dialectic of Apollo and Dionysus oscillates

2. Milbank, *Theology and Social Theory*, 434, 438.

3. David Bentley Hart, *The Beauty of the Infinite: The Aesthetics of Christian Truth*
(Grand Rapids: Eerdmans, 2004), 180. Compare Milbank, *Theology and Social
Theory*, 381: "As much as Deleuze, Christianity places in the *arche* (the Trinity) a
multiple which is not set dialectically over against the one, but itself manifests unity.
Unlike Deleuze, it is not still confined by the gigantic side of ancient myth, and shares
no taste for monstrosity."

without resolution between endless repetitions of the same emptiness, the same play of reflection and inversion.[4]

The distinctiveness of the Christian Trinity, he continues, is that it does not partake of this to and fro between sameness and difference, but rather composes a harmonic melody of unity and diversity in "the music of a triune God."[5]

Furthermore, Hart and Milbank insist that the relationship between Parmenidean unity and Heraclitean diversity in secular thought is characterized in terms of strife, war, and violence. Is this not a little too dramatic, though, going beyond what Deleuze himself says to paint his ontology as more agonistic than it really is? Deleuze's own language of becoming and difference would be violent only if it violated fixed identities and Forms that, on his account, are abstract fictions to begin with. Furthermore, he is at pains to stress that "one cannot over emphasize the extent to which the notions of struggle, war, rivalry or even comparison are foreign to Nietzsche and to his conception of the will to power," because for Nietzsche struggle belongs to the slaves who want to triumph over the strong, not the "active expression of forces" (*NaP*, 82). Deleuzian becoming is neither violent nor compassionate; it just is.

The charge that his thought manifests an "ontology of violence"[6] becomes more comprehensible, and a little more persuasive, when we view it as a claim not about Deleuze's thought in its own terms but about its interpretation from the point of view of Hart and Milbank's account of an alternative, Trinitarian difference, which "finds that the true form of difference is peace, of distance beauty."[7] When Trinitarian relationships are

4. Hart, *Beauty of the Infinite*, 151.
5. Hart, *Beauty of the Infinite*, 151.
6. Milbank, *Theology and Social Theory*, xx, 4; Hart, *Beauty of the Infinite*, 35–36.
7. Hart, *Beauty of the Infinite*, 178.

described in the Bible, they are overwhelmingly characterized as relationships of love, nowhere more repeatedly exemplified than in Jesus' Upper Room Discourse from John's Gospel: "Father, I desire that they also, whom you have given me, may be with me where I am, to see my glory that you have given me because you loved me before the foundation of the world" (John 17:24; cf. 14:31; 15:9; 17:23). God himself, as William Desmond notes, is a "community of agapeic service"[8] in which distance and difference do not engender strife and war, but bring forth mutual love. This emphasis on agapeic love is absent from Deleuze's account of difference, which is certainly closer to an ontology of strife than an ontology of love.

Finally, whereas Plato concocts a philosophy in order to construe identity as more primordial than difference, and whereas Deleuze reverses the priority in understanding identity to be a transient effect of an original difference, orthodox Christian theology insists on what has been called the *equal ultimacy* of the one and the many in the Trinity.[9] From this point of view, both unity and difference as construed by Plato and Deleuze are heretical and abstract oversimplifications that have forgotten their harmonious Trinitarian origins.

Christianity can speak of *difference*, as can, of course, Deleuze, but the term's meaning is radically dissimilar in each case because of the very different ontological contexts in which it arises. To fail to understand this is simply to equivocate on the term *difference*. It seems too hasty, then, for Simpson to argue that "here there are unrecognized affinities between Deleuze's pursuit of difference and Christian theology."[10] It cannot be the case that "there

8. William Desmond, *Ethics and the Between* (Albany, NY: SUNY Press, 2001), 483–514.

9. Cornelius Van Til, *The Defense of the Faith*, ed. K. Scott Oliphint, 4th ed. (Phillipsburg, NJ: P&R Publishing, 2008), 242.

10. Christopher Ben Simpson, *Deleuze and Theology* (London: Bloomsbury, 2012), 70.

is nothing theologically objectionable in, say, Deleuze's desire to speak of difference first and last, or his repeated insistence that there is nothing more 'true' than difference."[11] What is objectionable, theologically speaking, is the unproblematic reading across from Deleuze's very particular, ontological account of difference to Trinitarian equal ultimacy, with which it has precious little to do. To say anything else would be to fail to respect the distinctiveness of Deleuze, or of the Bible, or of both.

11. Hart, *Beauty of the Infinite*, 181–82.

5

CREATION AND TRANSCENDENCE

The second Deleuzian problem to consider is that of structure or order to which the transcendence of Plato's Forms is an answer. Deleuze is so opposed to the transcendence of the dogmatic image of thought, it will be remembered, because transcendence is no philosophical concept at all but a theological ruse of power introduced into philosophy by Plato in an attempt to preserve the iniquitous hierarchy of ancient society. The transcendent is privileged over the immanent, leading to an ascetic renunciation of this life in favor of another, supposedly higher world. Deleuze addresses the problem of order very differently, breaking the stranglehold of transcendence with his philosophy of immanence and thereby opening the way both to a philosophy free of theological influence and to a democratic society without the sort of rigid, elitist hierarchies fostered by transcendence (see *WIP*, 43–44, 86–88).

Nevertheless, Deleuze's philosophy of immanence privileges and affirms Plato's account of transcendence because it is this account and none other with which it engages and that it decisively rejects. It is Plato's transcendence that Deleuze casts as an oppressive guarantor of hierarchy that inevitably leads to a privileging of otherworldliness over this life and, in the final analysis, makes this life unreal and subjects it to what he calls "the great death" (*AO*, 334). The Bible, by contrast, thinks otherwise than both the transcendence that Plato affirms and the ontology of immanent becoming with which Deleuze replaces it.

From a biblical point of view, the oppression and nihilism that Deleuze wishes to overturn in his reversal of Platonism do not issue from transcendence per se but from the zero-sum opposition between transcendence and immanence that sucks all ultimate truth and meaning out of this world and installs a rigid hierarchy between otherworldly truth and this-worldly falsehood. What neither Plato nor Deleuze contemplates is a mediation of transcendence and immanence that disrupts the rigidly hierarchical relationship between them. It is just such a diagonalization of transcendence and immanence that emerges from the biblical account of creation. It is not that the Bible finds itself somewhere on the spectrum between Plato's affirmation of transcendence and Deleuze's pure immanence, much less that the Bible offers us nothing more than a "Platonism for the people."[1] The problem of transcendence and immanence does not pose itself in the same way within a biblical frame because there is no zero-sum game between transcendence and immanence: God is both radically immanent and utterly transcendent.

The biblical notion of transcendence does not sit God atop some Aristotelian great chain of being as the preeminent entity. As Hart explains, Christianity "for the first time confronted Western thought with a genuine discourse of transcendence, of

1. Friedrich Nietzsche, *Beyond Good and Evil: Prelude to a Philosophy of the Future*, ed. Rolf-Peter Horstmann and Judith Norman, trans. Judith Norman (Cambridge: Cambridge University Press, 2002), 4.

an ontological truth whose 'identity' is not completed by any ontic order of descent and ascent."[2] In one sense, the biblical God is more transcendent than Plato's Forms, for he cannot be considered part of the "all things" that exist; on the contrary, "by him all things were created, in heaven and on earth, visible and invisible, whether thrones or dominions or rulers or authorities—all things were created through him and for him" (Col. 1:16). God is not the highest being or the First Mover, such that it could make sense to create a hierarchy between God and creation: "He is not the high who stands over against the low, but is the infinite act of distance that gives high and low a place."[3] God does not rely on his creation in any way in order to be fully who God is (Acts 17:25), nor is he in competition with his creation. In Herbert McCabe's terms, "it is not possible that God and the universe should add up to make two."[4]

Yet it does not follow from this radical, nonhierarchical transcendence that God is far away, inhabiting another world that sucks the meaning out of this one. On the contrary, he is most radically immanent to his creation. He is the God in whom "we live and move and have our being" (Acts 17:28) and who "is actually not far from each one of us" (v. 27). The God who "upholds the universe by the word of his power" (Heb. 1:3) is not a remote deity. Augustine captures the radical transcendence and intimacy of the biblical God when he addresses his Creator as "more inward than my most inward part and higher than the highest element within me."[5] Is God immanent? More so than I am to myself.

2. David Bentley Hart, *The Beauty of the Infinite: The Aesthetics of Christian Truth* (Grand Rapids: Eerdmans, 2004), 130–31.

3. Hart, *Beauty of the Infinite*, 181.

4. Herbert McCabe, *God Matters* (London: Continuum, 2005), 6.

5. Augustine, *The Confessions*, trans. Henry Chadwick (Oxford: Oxford University Press, 2008), 43.

One important implication of this biblical account of immanence and transcendence is that, far from being a foundation for hierarchy and imperialism, God's absolute transcendence actively subverts them. God's kingship—as Nebuchadnezzar learns to his cost in the book of Daniel—does not provide a model for fragile human kingdoms, but relativizes them and deprives them of their legitimacy. Israel was granted a king not because then her earthly polity would finally and perfectly reflect God's heavenly reign, but against the advice of God's prophet Samuel, and out of an ungodly desire to have a king "that we also may be like all the nations" (1 Sam. 8:20). As for Christ, he affirms that "my kingdom is not of this world" (John 18:36), subverting any attempt to establish an earthly imperium[6] in his name. Far from being the blueprint for earthly despotism, God's kingship deprives it of any legitimate basis.

In addition, God's kingship leads directly to an equality of purpose among all created things, for all things are "for him [Christ]" (Col. 1:16) and all things glorify him (Ps. 19:1; 1 Cor. 15:39–41). This is not a subsumption of the difference of creation under the divine One, but a peaceful reconciliation of sameness and difference as "each instance of difference tells of God's glory, differently,"[7] and "every instance of being, as this particular being, equally declares God's glory."[8] There can be no substitution of one being for another, and no hierarchy of purpose: each instance of being relates directly to God in what we might call not a *flat ontology* but a *flat doxology* of glorifying God uniquely, irreplaceably, and distinctively. Intriguingly, Deleuze alludes to this biblical flatness in a short text entitled "Zones of Immanence" from 1985 (*2RM*, 261–64) in which he contrasts the Aristotelian great chain of being according to which "entities

---

6. Supreme power, absolute dominion.
7. Hart, *Beauty of the Infinite*, 296.
8. Hart, *Beauty of the Infinite*, 141.

have more or less being, more or less reality," with "a whole other inspiration" according to which

> Zones of immanence seemingly proliferate at the various stages or levels, even establishing connections between levels. In these Zones, Being is univocal, equal. In other words, every entity is equally being, in the sense that each actualizes its power in Immediate vicinity with the first cause. The distant cause is no more: rocks, flowers, animals, and humans equally celebrate the glory of God in a kind of crowned anarchy. (*2RM*, 261, translation altered)

Deleuze hastens to say that this affirmation of immanence is made in spite of, not because of, the "theological compromises" with which it is beset, and reveals "an internal atheism proper to" the love of God (*2RM*, 262). This leaves us with a very interesting and very important question (sadly, too complex to address in the present volume): is the biblical flat doxology that Deleuze acknowledges really, as he suggests, a corrupted echo of an atheistic immanence, or is his own immanence a corrupted version of biblical flat doxology? Furthermore, can such a question be answered in a noncircular way?[9]

9. These questions get to the heart of much of what is at stake in the conversation between theology and philosophy, but also risk, if posed crudely, descending into a fruitless battle for meaningless supremacy. I hope to devote a future book, necessarily longer than the present volume, to framing and addressing these and related questions.

6

SIN, NIHILISM, AND AFFIRMATION

As we move from creation to the account of the fall, we begin to see how the contours of biblical temporality shape a distinctive response to the problem of nihilism and affirmation. Once more, we start by noting something that Plato, Aristotle, and Deleuze have in common: an assumption that ethics and politics should be in conformity with a static ontology. This assumption has two elements. First, neither Deleuze nor his Greek interlocutors seek to decouple ontology from ethics; rather, they both (on Deleuze's account) reverse-engineer an ontology that will give them the politics they desire. None of them contemplates the possibility of a politics intentionally at variance with the way things are.

Second, for both Deleuze and Plato, the ontology that governs ethics and politics is temporally unchanging. Deleuze's ontology is, to be sure, one of becoming and change, but the conditions that govern that becoming do not themselves change. For Plato, the Forms are eternal, and there is no change over time in the nature of the relationship between Forms and their copies (see fig. 6.1). Similarly, for Deleuze, the virtual remains the virtual and the actual the actual, and though becoming always becomes differently, it is always becoming that becomes, and it never does anything other than become (see fig. 6.2). This is the sense in which both Plato's and Deleuze's ontologies are static: the structural relationship between ontology and ethics/politics remains constant in both cases. In addition, the structural relation between ontology and ethics/politics also remains unchanging over time. For Deleuze, ethics and politics will always be about becoming and difference because ontology will always be about becoming and difference. Similarly, for Plato, ethics and politics will always be about judgment and order because ontology will always be about judgment and order. Becoming is, was, and evermore shall be becoming, just as Plato's Forms are, were, and evermore shall be eternal.

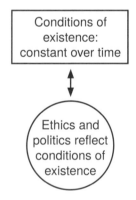

Fig. 6.1. In Platonic transcendence, ethics and politics reflect unchanging conditions of existence.

Given this shared assumption of a static ontology, Plato is construed as straightforwardly nihilistic with respect to valuing the eternal Forms over the decay and chance of this world, and Deleuze presents his own thought as straightforwardly

Fig. 6.2. In Deleuzian immanence, ethics and politics reflect unchanging conditions of existence.

affirmative of this world and of life. One can either deny this world and affirm a higher world or deny the very existence of a higher world in order to affirm this one. Once more, this world and eternity find themselves in a zero-sum opposition.

Sharing these assumptions with Plato as he does, Deleuze with his critique of the dogmatic image of thought can never be radical enough to address at the structural level the relationship between ontology and ethics. He is constrained to leave intact the logic that allows, for example, prerevolutionary France to read the preeminence of the "Sun King" Louis XIV from the celestial hierarchy: the heavenly bodies all orbit around one unique sun, so our society should accordingly be ordered around one unique King. This logic respects the same relationship between "how things are" in the world and "how things should be" in society, as Deleuze observes in his own thought. Why does it make any less sense to say that "we should have absolute monarchy because the sun is the center of the solar system" than it does to say that "difference is what there is; therefore, our politics should be a politics of difference"? How can such a position argue convincingly against a great chain of being that claims, "There is ontological hierarchy, so we should reflect that in our polity"? To respond with "no, there is no hierarchy, and we should reflect *that* in our polity" does nothing to disrupt the structure of the position; it merely challenges its contingent content. It does not amount to a radical rejection of the logic that makes possible the great chain of being. By changing his ontology rather than challenging the correspondence between ontology and politics per se, Deleuze does nothing to disrupt the deep logic of the dogmatic image of thought. What unites Deleuze and Plato/Aristotle here is more fundamental than what divides them.

A second problem with Deleuze's rejection of nihilism in favor of affirmation is that he finds himself constrained to embrace destruction in order to affirm becoming. In a universe governed by the law of the conservation of energy, the becoming of one instance of being requires the curtailment or even the death of others: many cells in my body must die in order for me to grow; plants and animals must die for me to live, either because I eat animals or because I sacrifice their potential habitat and possibilities to proliferate in order to harvest the vegetables and grains that I eat and to make a dwelling for myself; either my cancer dies or I do, and my viruses thrive and mutate at my expense; habitats are destroyed for nations to explore new ways of living; all too frequently, one nation or group has its possibilities of becoming curtailed in order that another's may proliferate; becoming on earth is bought at the expense of the slow dying of our sun. To affirm becoming is, as Hart argues at length, to affirm everything necessary for that becoming, and so to affirm death.[1]

---

1. Although he is right on this point, I believe Hart is mistaken—or at least misleading—when he ascribes to Deleuze "the affirmation of being in general." David Bentley Hart, *The Beauty of the Infinite: The Aesthetics of Christian Truth* (Grand Rapids: Eerdmans, 2004), 271. Deleuze is not constrained to affirm all being. Deleuze's Nietzsche affirms not *what* becomes, but the becoming of what becomes, and in so doing he maintains the ethical distinction between the *good* of healthy life and the *bad* of sickly life: "there is no Good or Evil in Nature in general, but there is

To embrace becoming is to embrace the destruction necessary for becoming, even if it is not to embrace destruction per se.

The Asymmetry of Good and Evil

So what would be a more radical approach? Could we simply say that ethics and politics are to be uncoupled holus-bolus from any ontology? That risks being just as uninteresting as shackling them to each other, and opens the door to arbitrariness and caprice. A more sophisticated approach would be to complexify the ethical and the political by introducing temporal development into the conditions that inform the relationship between ontology and ethics/politics. This is what we see in the biblical account.

The Bible, in fact, shares neither of the assumptions that Deleuze and Plato hold in common: that the conditions of existence informing nihilism and affirmation are unchanging, or that ethics and politics must be read directly off the current conditions of being. This is where the emplotted nature of the biblical account of reality begins to make a difference.[2] Creation and fall are not co-originary in the biblical account. The "it was very good" of Genesis 1 precedes the "cursed is the ground" of

---

goodness and badness, useful and harmful, for each existing mode" (*EPS*, 247), so sickness and death are bad for us because they thwart our immanent desire to increase our power to live and to explore new possibilities for living. To argue, with Hart, that "the game of Dionysus" is "one that can be played with equal elation and indifference in a summer meadow or a death camp" (*Beauty of the Infinite*, 271) assumes (1) that we can take a godlike position outside any consideration of what is useful or harmful for us, and (2) that the Nietzschean affirmation of the becoming of being overrides the Spinozan desire to increase one's power to act. Perhaps a more fruitful critique of Deleuze and Nietzsche here would question the rather convenient special pleading inherent in the claim that eternal return discriminates between becoming and identity: "why does only difference return?"

2. The term *emplotment* is central to Paul Ricœur's three-volume work *Time and Narrative*.

Genesis 3; God and the serpent are not two co-original, equal, and opposite deities, but the serpent is one of God's creatures (3:1) and bound by his curse (vv. 14–15). Similarly, there is an asymmetry of blessing and sin for Adam and Eve. God did not say, "Let us make sinners," but "Let us make man in our image" (1:26), and there is no indication that this image is negated by sin: if it were, why would God continue to communicate with Adam and Eve in a special way, make promises to them, and make them garments after the fall? Why, ultimately, would he send his Son to die for Adam and Eve's descendants?

Whereas God blesses Adam and Eve directly in Genesis 1:28, he does not curse them directly.[3] Both good and evil are present after Genesis 3, but they are present asymmetrically. Evil is not originary, and it will not persist forever. As Paul Ricoeur puts it, "The etiological myth of Adam is the most extreme attempt to separate the origin of evil from the origin of the good; its intention is to set up a radical origin of evil distinct from the more primordial origin of the goodness of things."[4] What is more, the event of evil does not negate the goodness of Genesis 1 and 2: Adam and Eve do not cease to be in God's image; the trees do not cease to produce their fruit; animals do not cease to reproduce according to their kind; and Adam and Eve do not cease to fill the earth and subdue it. All these aspects of God's good creation are marred by sin, but none are negated. There is, then, a crucial asymmetry between creation and fall in Genesis 1–3.

In addition, there are two hints already in Genesis 3 that the entry of sin into the world is not the final chapter in God's plan, in the same way that it was not the first. First of all, the

3. God does not use the word *curse* with Eve at all, and to Adam he says, "Cursed is the ground because of you" (Gen. 3:17). This is in pointed distinction to the serpent, to whom God says, "Cursed are you above all livestock" (v. 14).

4. Paul Ricoeur, *The Symbolism of Evil* (Boston: Beacon Press, 1967), 233.

protevangelium of Genesis 3:15[5] hints at the ultimate overcoming of Satan through Eve's offspring, Christ, and his death on the cross. The protevangelium also introduces the temporality of promise that structures biblical time and means that a biblical outlook can never merely straightforwardly affirm or deny the present. Second, God's killing of an animal in order to make garments for Adam and Eve (3:21) has been read as a foreshadowing of the sacrificial system that will culminate in the defeat of sin and death at the cross. Hart expresses this radical asymmetry with the image of a palimpsest:

> Christian thought expects to find in every cultural coding a fundamental violence; no primordial innocence is displaced by the archive; but, perhaps fantastically, it treats this pervasive violence, inscribed upon being's fabric, as a palimpsest, obscuring another text that is still written (all created being is "written") but in the style of a letter declaring love.[6]

At every point, then, evil is overwriting but not destroying a more primordial and enduring message of blessing and love; at every point it is temporally bounded, framed, and relativized by an original creation and a promise of redemption. Genesis 3 is certainly the chapter that announces the great disaster, but at the same time it works extraordinarily hard to limit evil, to say that it is not ultimate, that it has a beginning in history and that it is not a feature of humanity as originally created, however inveterate and inescapable it may be for the time being. This means that a biblical attitude to this world can be one neither of simple affirmation nor of straightforward denial.

---

5. God to the serpent: "I will put enmity between you and the woman, and between your offspring and her offspring; he shall bruise your head, and you shall bruise his heel."

6. Hart, *Beauty of the Infinite*, 55.

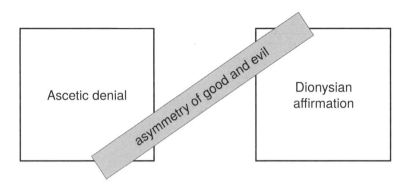

Fig. 6.3. The biblical asymmetry of good and evil diagonalizes the asceticism of Deleuze's dogmatic image of thought and his own Dionysian affirmation.

The Christian apologist Francis Schaeffer used a musical metaphor to communicate this biblical asymmetry of good and evil:

> *The Christian world view can be divided into what I call a major and a minor theme....*
>
> First, the *minor theme* is the abnormality of the revolting world.... There is a defeated and sinful side to the Christian's life. If we are at all honest, we must admit that in this life there is no such thing as totally victorious living. In every one of us there are those things which are sinful and deceiving and, while we may see substantial healing, in this life we do not come to perfection.
>
> The *major theme* is the opposite of the minor; it is the meaningfulness and purposefulness of life.... So therefore the major theme is an optimism in the area of being; everything is not absurd, there is meaning.[7]

---

7. Francis Schaeffer, *Art and the Bible* (Leicester: Inter-Varsity Press, 2009), 83–84.

There is futility, and there is meaning and goodness, but they are not equal and opposite realities: goodness precedes, exceeds, and succeeds sin; it is the major theme to sin's minor theme.

So to draw a Christian ethics and politics out of our present conditions of existence would be to unpardonably collapse the temporally distended biblical emplotment of the relationship between good and evil. It would collapse the asymmetrical relationship between the "it was very good" and "cursed is the ground because of you" in Genesis 1–3, and it would collapse the temporality of promise initiated in the protevangelium. Both the nihilism that Deleuze rejects and his own Nietzschean ethic of affirmation fail to grapple with this emplotted biblical account.

Emplotted Biblical Ethics and Politics

In a biblical frame, we cannot read off from the way things are now to the way they should be; we must locate ourselves in an unfolding story that weaves a complex set of evolving relationships between good and evil. A Christian whose thinking is patterned according to the shape of the biblical narrative will be neither an Eeyore nor a Tigger, neither a Cassandra nor a Pollyanna. Both affirmation and denial have their place, but they are not symmetrical. In fact, because sin does not completely destroy anything in creation, everything is affirmed in its goodness, nothing is denied outright, and everything will be changed and transfigured as it is brought under Christ (Eph. 1:10). Oliver O'Donovan powerfully makes this point toward the end of his *Resurrection and Moral Order*, when he argues that God's *yes* to humankind in Christ is not in any way compromised by his *no* to rebellion:

> In accepting [Christ], God has accepted mankind totally, and the created universe with mankind. In rejecting all that rejects

him, God has rejected nothing of mankind and nothing of the created universe, but only that which denies and detracts from them. No act that is performed, no life that is lived in refusal of what God has done, has any claim upon him—not even the claim that if he will not capitulate to it on its own terms, something will be lacking from his restored creation.[8]

There is indeed a denial that is central to the Christian story, but it is not the denial of this world. It is the denial of denial itself, the denial of that which, in denying God, would deny the fullness of humankind and of creation.

Genesis 3, then, intervenes into the conversation between Deleuze and Plato on denial and affirmation in two ways. First, it diagonalizes denial and affirmation through the asymmetry of good and evil in its temporally distended emplotment of creation and fall (see fig. 6.3), and it brings the whole of biblical emplotment to bear on any ethics and politics that would be drawn from it, which avoids the need to draw ethical or political principles exclusively from the current situation. To elaborate a Christian politics is to plot its contours (its understanding of power, institutions, the common good, and sovereignty, to name but some of the most important elements) in terms of an emplotted biblical theology summarized in the fourfold schema of creation, fall, redemption, and consummation (see fig. 6.4).

In the complex foldings, promises, and memories at the heart of the emplotted biblical temporality of creation, fall, redemption, and consummation, all four of these turning points inform ethics and politics right here and right now, but not symmetrically and not in a way insensitive to temporal development through the stages of salvation history. As we will see when we

---

8. Oliver O'Donovan, *Resurrection and Moral Order* (Leicester: Inter-Varsity Press, 1986), 256.

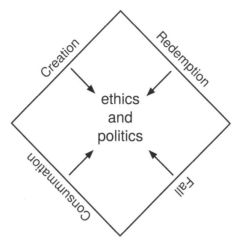

Fig. 6.4. Emplotted Biblical Ethics and Politics

discuss *eschatological realism* below, if anything, it is the radical transformation of the eschaton that is normative ethically and politically, not the current period of the "last days."

Renunciation, Affirmation, and Doxological Dispossession

The Bible also diagonalizes the dichotomy of self-denial and self-affirmation in its anthropology. For the Augustine of the *Confessions*, God is "more inward than my most inward part and higher than the highest element within me,"[9] and Augustine discovers who he is and finds his sense of self only through the self-forgetfulness that comes with reaching out to God in praise. Similarly, Thomas's insistence "the esse of creatures is an esse-ad-creatorem (their to-be is to-be-towards-the-creator)" is one that "utterly transforms Aristotle's world, where the hallmark of

9. Augustine, *The Confessions*, trans. Henry Chadwick (Oxford: Oxford University Press, 2008), 43.

substance is to 'exist in itself.'"[10] Augustine's and Thomas's account of self, as well as the self of the New Testament, is not self-contained and stable but Godward and ecstatic (from the prefix *ek-*, "out" or "out from," and *stasis*, "standing" or "position"). As Hart rightly points out, there is no stable, self-contained subject in orthodox Christian theology.[11] What we have instead is, in Michael Hanby's terms, a "doxological self constituted through its participation in the delight shared between the Father and the Son and in the unity of Christ's one body, human and divine."[12] Such a self is gathered only as it moves outside and beyond itself in worship to its Creator, and can therefore never be closed in on itself.

This doxological, ecstatic self is important for our reflections in this present section because it diagonalizes Deleuze's opposition between the self-denial and self-renunciation of transcendence and the ethic of immanence consisting in maximizing one's own power to act.

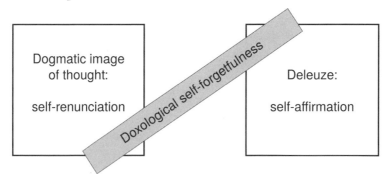

Fig. 6.5. Doxological self-forgetfulness diagonalizes the ascetic self-renunciation of the dogmatic image of thought and Deleuze's Nietzschean affirmation.

---

10. David Burrell, "Providence," in *The Cambridge Companion to the Summa Theologiae* (Cambridge: Cambridge University Press, 2016), 165.

11. Hart, *Beauty of the Infinite*, 114–15.

12. Michael Hanby, *Augustine and Modernity* (London: Routledge, 2003), 74.

Both self-renunciation and self-maximization maintain a focus on the self that is loosened and disrupted in the self-forgetfulness of a biblical "doxological dispossession."[13] If the perverse logic of self-renunciation is "he who loses his life will lose it," and the logic of the maximization of potential is "he who saves his life will save it," then the doxologically dispossessed self follows the paradoxical biblical pattern that "whoever would save his life will lose it, but whoever loses his life for my sake will find it" (Matt. 16:25). It is crucial to note the asymmetry between losing and saving in this verse. Matthew does not write "whoever loses his life will find it," but he introduces an outward focus in the second part of the verse that is not there in the self-referential reflexivity of the first part: "for my sake." The addition of these words turns the verse from a perverse exaltation of self-destruction to an ecstatic Christward doxology.[14]

13. Hanby, *Augustine and Modernity*, 24.
14. The logic of self-forgetfulness is explored at greater length in Timothy Keller, *The Freedom of Self-Forgetfulness: The Path to True Christian Joy* (Leyland, UK: 10Publishing, 2012).

7

INCARNATION, ACTUALITY, AND VIRTUALITY

The next key moment in the mythos of biblical theology that repays consideration in relation to Deleuze's thought is the incarnation, which gives us a distinctively biblical set of reflections on the problem of how to relate our experience of the world to its condition of possibility—in other words, to what lies behind it or makes it possible. Plato relates our experience to its condition of possibility by arguing that the changeable, decaying world we experience is made sense of through the eternal Forms that we can only intuit intellectually. Deleuze understands the relation in terms of the actual and the virtual in what he calls his *transcendental empiricism*, inferring the conditions of experience (= transcendental) from the world as we experience it (= empiricism).

What Plato and Deleuze share, in this case, is a conviction that the condition of possibility of our experience (the Forms and the virtual, respectively) is not immediately apprehensible within experience itself. I never see or touch the Forms directly (see fig. 7.1), nor do I experience the virtual directly (see fig. 7.2).

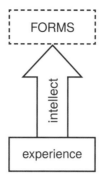

Fig. 7.1. Plato understands the transcendent condition of experience through the intellect.

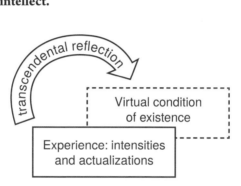

Fig. 7.2. Deleuze understands the immanent condition of experience through transcendental reflection.

Plato and Deleuze also share the view that we accede to the condition of our experience by a particular form of reflection from within our experience. In both cases, the direction of movement is from inside to outside experience, either through the intellect (Plato) or through transcendental reflection (Deleuze).

Once again, the Bible cuts across this shared assumption with the claim that at a particular moment in history, the condition of possibility of our existence became apprehensible within the world of experience: the incarnation of Jesus the Christ. It does so, in fact, in terms of a threefold scandal, at least to the abstract universalizing spirit of the Enlightenment, which Plato helped shape and which Deleuze substantially (though not wholly) shares: the scandal of the particular, the scandal of the historical, and the scandal of the material.[1] On the biblical account, the direction of epistemological travel is not from the inside of experience to the outside, but outside in (see fig. 7.3).

Fig. 7.3. The Word became flesh.

The Scandal of the Particular

The first scandal of the incarnation is the scandal of the particular.[2] In Christianity, the condition of possibility of our

1. Although these three scandals can be traced throughout the whole biblical emplotment, I have chosen to address them in relation to the incarnation because, first, the incarnation presents an instance of all three scandals together and, second, the incarnation is a particularly intense and biblically elaborated moment for all three.

2. *Scandal of the particular*, or *scandal of particularity*, is a term frequently used by contemporary theologians to refer to the claim that one particular man, Jesus Christ, is the Savior for all. It translates the German *Ärgernis der Einmaligkeit*, first used by Gerhard Kittel in "The Jesus of History," in *Mysterium Christi: Christological Studies by British and German Theologians*, ed. Gerhard Kittel, G. K. A. Bell, and A. Deissman

existence is revealed not as an abstract, universal principle, but as a particular person: Jesus Christ. Note that Christ is not merely the one *in* or *through* whom revelation takes place, as if he were the mouthpiece or conduit for an abstract reality beyond his own person. This would be characteristic of the Christ of the Enlightenment, not of the Christ of the Bible. In his *Groundwork of the Metaphysics of Morals*, for example, Immanuel Kant holds that "even the Holy One of the Gospel must first be compared with our idea of moral perfection before he is recognized as [a model]."[3] Christ, for Kant, is the embodiment of an abstract idea more fundamental than the particular person of Christ himself. The language of the Bible, by contrast, will not allow us to frame Christ as an intermediary or vessel for a deeper, impersonal reality. Christ *is* the truth: "Jesus said to him, 'I am the way, and the truth, and the life. No one comes to the Father except through me'" (John 14:6). This identification of Christ with, rather than as a mere ambassador for, the condition of our existence is further stressed by Paul in Colossians 1:

> He is the image of the invisible God, the firstborn of all creation. For by him all things were created, in heaven and on earth, visible and invisible, whether thrones or dominions or rulers or authorities—all things were created through him and for him. And he is before all things, and in him all things hold together. (Col. 1:15–17)

(London: Longmans, 1930), 31. In what follows, I have sought to clarify the overlapping ideas often gathered under the umbrella of the *scandal of particularity* by separating the scandal of the particular (that Christ was a specific man), of the historical (that he was born at a specific time and place), and of the material (that he had a body).

3. Immanuel Kant, *Groundwork of the Metaphysics of Morals*, trans. Mary Gregor and Jens Timmermann, Cambridge Texts in the History of Philosophy (Cambridge: Cambridge University Press, 2012), 23.

Christ does not only tell us of the one by whom all things were created; he is that one. He does not only explain how all things hold together; he is the one in whom all things hold together. In other words, nothing in Christ's particularity invalidates his universality; to think so is to continue to labor under the Enlightenment prejudice that assumes that the ultimate and the universal must necessarily be abstract and impersonal. "In Christian thought," by contrast, "the 'transcendent' vantage that takes in all things is that provided by a particular first-century Jew."[4] Note also that in John 14, the one about whom Christ bears witness is no more abstract than he is himself. Jesus does not say, "Whoever has seen me has seen the ground of being," or "Whoever has seen me has seen the ultimate reality of the universe," but "Whoever has seen me has seen the Father" (John 14:9).

This particularity does not mean that the Father or Christ ceases to be universal; to assume so would once again be to fall under the Enlightenment prejudice. The particular Christ, Jesus of Nazareth, is universal; the particular Father, the "God and Father of our Lord Jesus Christ" (e.g., Eph. 1:3), is universal.[5] This concrete particularity of Christ sits in contrast to the Deleuzian virtual, the transcendental condition of being, which remains inaccessible to direct experience. Christianity transgresses the distinction between particulars and their transcendental or transcendent condition that both Plato and Deleuze maintain and on which they both rely.

4. David Bentley Hart, *The Beauty of the Infinite: The Aesthetics of Christian Truth* (Grand Rapids: Eerdmans, 2004), 321.

5. It would be too weak to claim that Christ is merely a *concrete universal*. Though Hegel does introduce the notion of the concrete universal to counter the prejudice that the universal must always be only abstract, concrete universals (such as *human*) can be instantiated in any number of different individuals and so are not an equivalent to the incarnation's scandal of particularity.

The Scandal of the Historical

The second scandal of the incarnation is the scandal of the historical. The Bible claims not that the incarnation instantiates an eternal relationship between God and his creation, nor that it illustrates an unchanging reality, but that it is a one-time event that took place at a particular moment in calendar history—an event, indeed, that cleaves calendar history in two. The incarnation is irreducibly historical: Christ is not an abstract eternal reality but has a particular human genealogy, being "descended from David according to the flesh" (Rom. 1:3).

In the prologue to his Gospel, John presents the incarnation in three moments of increasing intensity:

> The light shines in the darkness . . . . The true light, which gives light to everyone, was coming into the world. . . . And the Word became flesh and dwelt among us, and we have seen his glory, glory as of the only Son from the Father, full of grace and truth. (John 1:5, 9, 14)

In addition to the progressive accumulation of detail about the incarnation across these three verses, I would like to alight particularly on their sequence of tenses. John 1:5 contains the present indicative active verb *phainei*, "is appearing" or "is shining." The present is continuous, with the sense that "shining in the darkness is what the light does," rather than pointing to a temporally punctual event ("right here and now, the light is shining in the darkness"). There is as yet no indication of historical specificity: this tense could describe the relationship between Platonic Forms and particulars ("the particulars participate in the Forms") or the Deleuzian actual and virtual ("entities in our experience are actualizations of the virtual"). In verse 9, however, we begin to see the contours of historical specificity emerge: the true light "was coming" (*erchomenon*) into the world, a verb in the aorist tense, middle voice, which could be translated as either "is coming" or "was coming." In either case, the tense indicates that the relationship between the Word and the world is not eternally unchanging: something happens. This emerging specificity is sharpened even further in verse 14: "the Word *became* flesh and dwelt among us, and we *have seen* his glory."[6] "Became" translates the second aorist *egeneto*: something happened in the past, continued for an unspecified length of time, and has now finished happening. It is followed by two additional aorist verbs: "dwelt" (*eskenosen*) and "have seen" (*etheasametha*, aorist middle voice). *Eskenosen* derives from the Greek *skene*, meaning "booth" or "tabernacle," underlining not only the temporal but the spatial specificity of the incarnation: Christ's incarnation is not an abstract or general indwelling, but, like the Old Testament tabernacle—or indeed like any other tent—is pitched at a particular location for a particular length of time. As philosopher Slavoj Žižek rightly notes, Christianity is unique in that it "offers Christ as a mortal-temporal individual, and insists that belief in the temporal event of Incarnation is the only path to eternal truth and salvation."[7]

The incarnation, in short, is not an eternal reality or a timeless spiritual truth; it was an event. There was a moment when it began, a period of time when Christ was incarnate on earth, and a moment when he ceased to be so. The incarnation is emplotted in biblical history. I use the term *event* here with its full philosophical weight. An event is something that happens, often unexpectedly or unforeseeably, to disrupt the natural development of already-existing realities and the extrapolation

6. The other verb in most English translations, "dwelt" in the ESV, translates the noun *eskenosen*, "booths" or "tabernacles."

7. Slavoj Žižek, *The Fragile Absolute: Or Why the Christian Legacy Is Worth Fighting For* (London: Verso, 2001), 96.

of already-existing conditions, something contingent and unpredictable that creates a *before* and an *after* and that therefore makes history itself possible. Revelation is an event in this sense because it interrupts the regular and predictable outworking of natural processes,[8] as Oliver O'Donovan explains:

> Any philosophy of history which takes some other starting-point than simple revelation is doomed to end up trapped within one or another form of natural determinism. It can give no account of the future except by extrapolating regularities from the past. There are, of course, many possible regularities for it to choose among, so that there are many different types of philosophy of history. Some are cyclical, singling out the repetitive character of the natural processes and extending the principle of repetition explicitly to include larger patterns of events; in which case they are, in the end, quite overtly philosophies of nature. . . . To be truly "history," history must be shaped by the unique, by that which cannot be guessed from the scrutiny of natural repetitions.[9]

So while it is not incorrect to say that the incarnation is an event in history, it is also correct to say that history itself, emplotment itself, is made possible by revelatory events such as the incarnation. Emplotted revelation is the condition of possibility of history (in O'Donovan's strong sense of the term *history*), as well as itself partaking in the scandal of the historical.[10]

---

8. Though these "natural processes" are also themselves, of course, sustained second by second by God.

9. Oliver O'Donovan, *Resurrection and Moral Order* (Leicester: Inter-Varsity Press, 1986), 82–83.

10. This also helps us to see why O'Donovan, perhaps surprisingly, associates Christ's particularity with his divine nature, and his universality with his human nature (see *Resurrection and Moral Order*, 143–44). The divine is the locus of the unique, the irreplaceable, the particular, and the human is the locus of the universal, the

The Scandal of the Material

The third and final scandal of the incarnation is the scandal of the material: Christ came not as a pure idea but with a normal body with all its normal limitations and functions. For those who labor under the Enlightenment prejudice that ultimate reality must be pure, abstract, and universal, the notion that God could have a body is indeed a scandal.

In the terms of the prologue to John's Gospel, the Word did not become idea or language, but "flesh" (John 1:14): blood, bone, and sinews, inscribing a scandal of the material at the heart of biblical emplotment. John emphasizes this carnality at the beginning of his first letter:

> That which was from the beginning, which we have heard, which we have seen with our eyes, which we looked upon and have touched with our hands, concerning the word of life— the life was made manifest, and we have seen it, and testify to it and proclaim to you the eternal life, which was with the Father and was made manifest to us—that which we have seen and heard we proclaim also to you. (1 John 1:1–3)

"That which was from the beginning" and "the eternal life, which was with the Father," is the same as that which, in a crescendo of three sensory encounters of increasing proximity, "we have heard, . . . seen[,] . . . touched."

---

representative, the relative: "As the Lord of time [Christ] confers unique significance on each moment, fashioning time into history; as a participant in time he stands in relation to other moments in time as they stand in relation to each other and to his moment" (*Resurrection and Moral Order*, 144). What O'Donovan shows us here is, crucially, why the incarnation of Christ is not merely one instance of the instantiation of the representation of a universal in a particular, but the unique instance of "the coming within universal order of that which belongs outside it, the one divine Word which gave it its origin and which pronounces its judgment" (*Resurrection and Moral Order*, 144).

The incarnation is not just a scandal of the material in the sense that Christ had a physical body, however. It vindicates and dignifies the whole material world, as Hart explains: "the incarnation of the Logos, the infinite ratio of all that is, reconciles us not only to God, but to the world, by giving us back a knowledge of creation's goodness."[11] That God should become flesh reiterates the "it was good" pronounced on the material world in Genesis 1; that he should further be raised and ascend with a body of flesh after his death seals the importance of the material for eternity: "the resurrection of Christ directs our attention back to the creation which it vindicates."[12] The Gnosticism that Deleuze rightly rejects preaches a redemption from creation, but biblical Christianity preaches the redemption of creation.

As with all three scandals discussed in this section, the incarnation is but one instance of the biblical scandal of the material among many. This scandal runs from the "it was very good" pronounced on the material creation in Genesis 1:31 through the bodily resurrection of Christ, to the materiality of the new heavens and the new earth at the end of the book of Revelation. The compound effect of this repeated insistence on the goodness of matter from Genesis to Revelation lends weight to Archbishop William Temple's claim that Christianity "is the most avowedly materialist of the great religions."[13]

This Christian vindication of materiality stands once more in contrast to both Plato and Deleuze. It would be anathema to Plato's system to suggest that we could hear, see, or touch the Forms, for "the very being with which true knowledge is concerned" is "the colorless, shapeless, intangible Being that truly is, perceptible only to the soul's pilot, intelligence, which is the

11. Hart, *Beauty of the Infinite*, 133.
12. O'Donovan, *Resurrection and Moral Order*, 31.
13. William Temple, *Nature, Man, and God* (Edinburgh: T&T Clark, 1934), 478.

object of the class of true knowledge."[14] Similarly, the Deleuzian virtual by definition cannot be directly apprehended by the senses. What Plato and Deleuze both put asunder, the Bible joins together (see fig. 7.4).

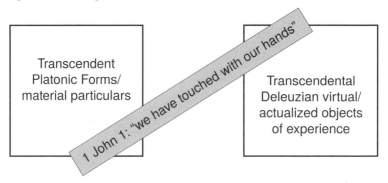

Fig. 7.4. The incarnation diagonalizes Plato and Deleuze's account of the relationship between experience and its condition.

The scandals of the particular, the historical, and the material mean that the Christian need not look beyond this world to apprehend its ground. Christ, unlike Platonic Forms, could be heard, seen, and touched. He cannot be touched now because, as befits a historical event as opposed to an abstract, eternal reality, Christ came at a particular point in history. Christ, unlike the virtual, is not the transcendental condition of possibility of the actual, a necessary inference from the way things are, but one who "dwelt among us" such that "we have seen his glory" (John 1:14), not heard a report of his glory or seen it reenacted as in a play.

Because of the scandals of the historical, the material, and the particular, it is rather misleading to claim that Christianity has, or is, a metanarrative. A metanarrative is an explanation of the

14. Plato, *Phaedrus*, ed. Harvey Yunis, Cambridge Greek and Latin Classics (Cambridge: Cambridge University Press, 2011), 141.

world that sits not on the surface of events but beyond (*meta*) the history that it attempts to frame and the interventions that it aims to legitimize. Like Deleuze's virtual, it is an inference from the way things are, not directly visible on the surface of those things themselves. In the light of the three scandals enumerated in this section, it would be more appropriate, in the case of the Bible, to prefer the prefix *meso-* (from *mesos*, meaning "middle" or "between" or "amid") and speak of the Christian mesonarrative of the Christ who "dwelt among us." Ultimate reality is manifest in the midst of events, in Christ's sinewy flesh, at a particular moment in history, rather than on a "meta" level of abstract explanation separate from those particular, historical, material events themselves.

8

JUDGMENT, MINORITARIANISM, AND GRACE

Judgment

The next problem around which we can bring Deleuze and the Bible into conversation is that of judgment and discrimination. Judging between true and false copies is at the heart of Plato's ontology and politics, but for Deleuze, such judgment—which he pejoratively labels the *judgment of God*—is intensely problematic because it constrains and oppresses the free becoming of simulacra. Plato and Deleuze share what I propose to call an unbroken linearity of positive and negative valuation: judgment draws a line between one sort of entity or event that is positively valued (the "true" copies of Platonic Forms for Plato or the becoming of simulacra for Deleuze) and a second sort that are negatively valued ("false" simulacra for Plato or the so-called "true" copies that Deleuze denounces). *Linearity* refers to the idea that, for both Plato and Deleuze, the positively valued remains positively valued, and the negative remains negative, in the manner of two parallel lines receding into the distance and never meeting.

We saw above that the only way Deleuze can see to avoid the oppressive effects of transcendence is to excise transcendence from his ontology altogether. In a similar fashion, his response to the problem of judging between the true and the false is to have done with the true altogether. Once again, this does nothing to disrupt or subvert the logic of judgment itself: in eliminating the true from his thought, Deleuze tacitly admits that judgment can only be authoritarian and oppressive in the way he understands it in Plato.

Minoritarianism

To explore in more detail how Deleuze seeks to respond to the problem of discriminating judgment, let us return to his minoritarian politics outlined above. According to the majoritarian paradigm, the privileged group (say: white, European heterosexual Anglo-Saxon Protestant males) is positively valued and becomes the norm against which all other groups are measured and—inevitably—found wanting. Deleuze attacks this hierarchical judgment through his minoritarian politics, which does not simply reverse the roles and privilege a "minority" over the "majority" group, but picks away at the very idea of fixed group identities on which majoritarian politics relies. Nevertheless, despite disrupting majoritarian categories in this way, it is extremely difficult for Deleuze to free himself from the positive and negative valuations of discriminating judgment. The majoritarian becomes the negatively valued term, and the minoritarian the positively valued.

Or take another example: Deleuze's repeated assertion that he is elaborating an ethics that is beyond good and evil (see, for example, *DR*, 6; *WIP*, 72; *PI*, 29), where *good* and *evil* are a transcendent moral opposition imposed on life from the outside, as opposed to the immanent ethical difference of *good* and *bad*, which arises within life itself and "provides the basis for a real ethical difference, which we must substitute for a false moral opposition" (*EPS*, 254). Even if this distinction removes transcendent values from ethics (which I think is an open question, but not my argument here), it still maintains the distinction between one straightforwardly positively valued term (*good*) and one straightforwardly negatively valued term (*bad*). Furthermore, moving beyond good and evil becomes the new good, and not moving beyond good and evil becomes the new bad (or evil; the distinction does not matter for the purposes of this argument). As a result, the nefarious effects of discriminating judgment persist, for the one who is beyond good and evil now looks down on and condemns those who still operate within the categories of good and evil, just as the enlightened philosopher who can tell the difference between true and false copies looks down on and condemns the sophist who cannot or will not do so. Different players, same game. In this sense, Deleuze's overturning of Platonism is still *linear*: a positively valued position and a negatively valued position still emerge in his thought, despite his disruption of Platonic categories of true and false copy, and these positively and negatively valued positions are not themselves disrupted or overturned (see figs. 8.1, 8.2).

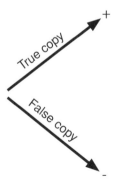

Fig. 8.1. Plato's Linear Account of the Ethics of the True and False Copy

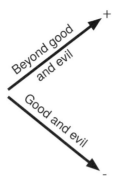

Fig. 8.2. Deleuze's Linear Account of an Ethics beyond Good and Evil

Grace

The Bible also seeks to disrupt and subvert stable categories of discriminating judgment, but it does so in a different way from Deleuze. The doctrine of grace offers a different response to the problem of discrimination because it rethinks judgment in a way that breaks the linearity of positive and negative valuation. To see how grace disrupts the linearity of judgment, let us examine Paul's famous discussion of grace in Ephesians 2:1–10:

And you were dead in the trespasses and sins in which you once walked, following the course of this world, following the prince of the power of the air, the spirit that is now at work in the sons of disobedience—among whom we all once lived in the passions of our flesh, carrying out the desires of the body and the mind, and were by nature children of wrath, like the rest of mankind. But God, being rich in mercy, because of the great love with which he loved us, even when we were dead in our trespasses, made us alive together with Christ—by grace you have been saved—and raised us up with him and seated us with him in the heavenly places in Christ Jesus, so that in the coming ages he might show the immeasurable riches of his grace in kindness toward us in Christ Jesus. For by grace you have been saved through faith. And this is not your own doing; it is the gift of God, not a result of works, so that no one may boast. For we are his workmanship, created in Christ Jesus for good works, which God prepared beforehand, that we should walk in them.

Paul's dramatic use of the language of death in verse 1 sets the scene for the nonlinearity or *great reversal*[1] that is to characterize salvation in this passage. Death is the epitome of passivity, a state from which it is impossible to emerge through any linear intention and execution of an action. If this state is to be altered, then it must be altered from outside; the dead are denuded of any possibility of intervening in their own situation.

The "but God" of Ephesians 2:4 signals a change in the subject of the passage's verbs, from humanity in verses 1–3 to God in verses 4–10, and the passive voice in "by grace you have been saved" (v. 5) is crucial for Paul's account of salvation and for the distinctiveness of nonlinear grace. This change of subject signals that in Paul's eyes, all that humanity actively contributes to its salvation is the "trespasses and sins" from which it needs to be saved, and salvation itself is God's doing. Salvation in this passage is not the accomplishment of a human plan. It is an "event" in the strong, philosophical sense described above, a moment of nonlinear rupture that cannot be accounted for in terms of the extrapolation of factors already present in the situation. Salvation requires an intervention from outside.

In Ephesians 2:4–5, Paul stresses that new life is given by God "because of the great love with which he loved us, even when we were dead in our trespasses." Paul ensures here, by

---

1. I discuss the motif of the *great reversal* at length in *Michel Foucault*, Great Thinkers (Phillipsburg, NJ: P&R Publishing, 2018), 79–82.

juxtaposing these two clauses, that the sufficient reason for salvation is located in God and not in humanity. God is not compelled to save in response to any trait or quality of humanity, but is led to save by his own love; he is not compelled by our pleading, for we—Paul once again stresses—are dead.

In Ephesians 2:8, Paul closes off the last possible avenue for boasting that salvation might offer. Surely, it might be objected, I can take some modest pride in realizing that I needed to be saved, in repenting, and in putting my faith in God that he might save me, not relying on my own works. Paul forecloses this possibility by including faith itself in the category of things that are "not your own doing" and "the gift of God." The gift of repentance and faith is itself, furthermore, a nonlinear rupture rather than the smooth following through of a premeditated plan or intention. As Oliver O'Donovan describes in *Resurrection and Moral Order*, repentance requires "a detachment of the will from its self-chosen orientation," and it "cannot be the mere realignment of a will that retains a fundamental continuity with its past; it involves a moment of self-annihilation."[2] These, then, are the two senses in which grace is nonlinear: it requires a rupture of the linear sequence of intentions and actions with an intervention from outside, and it detaches or uncouples the will from its self-chosen orientation.

The conclusion of Paul's argument is emphatic: "no one may boast" (Eph. 2:9). To be saved by grace is to undercut any possibility of legitimately looking down on the unsaved, as though one's own wisdom, integrity, strength, or faith were to thank for one's salvation. It undercuts any possibility of erecting a hierarchy of merit with the saved on top and the unsaved at the bottom. To be saved by grace is to recognize that any such

2. Oliver O'Donovan, *Resurrection and Moral Order* (Leicester: Inter-Varsity Press, 1986), 112–13.

hierarchy is a perversion and caricature of salvation. The philosopher condemns the sophist; the minoritarian condemns the majoritarian; the one who is beyond good and evil condemns the one who is not; but for the one saved by grace, the possibility of boasting in his or her position is radically undercut. If I am saved by grace, then I must by definition acknowledge that any standing I have is a gift from God, and that all I contributed to my salvation is the sin from which I needed rescue; to suggest anything else is to deny grace. Grace defangs the hierarchization implicit in discriminating judgment, and places the saved under precisely the disapprobation reserved in linear hierarchies for the negatively valued group, delegitimizing linear hierarchies in the process (see fig. 8.3).

Note that grace does not eliminate judgment altogether. Those who are saved by grace are still saved, and those who are not saved are still not saved. What it eliminates is the possibility of those who are saved by grace using that fact as a means of creating a hierarchy with themselves on the top and the unsaved at the bottom. In other words, it subverts the danger of discriminating judgment not by seeking to eliminate judgment per se but by undermining the hierarchies to which judgment dangerously predisposes.

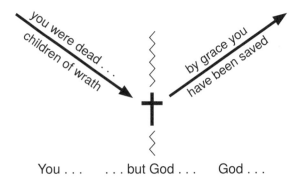

Fig. 8.3. The Nonlinearity of Biblical Grace from Ephesians 2

Is there not a sense, though, in which Deleuze's minoritarian politics is also delegitimizing? Yes, there is: becoming-woman is not a stable identity; insofar as it is minoritarian at all, it is open, fluid, continually becoming, and never self-affirming or self-congratulatory: minoritarian politics is not the equal and opposite of majoritarian. There is still a difference between Deleuzian minoritarianism and biblical grace, however. The difference is that Deleuze's oppositions (such as that between minoritarian and majoritarian, or between the rhizomatic and the arborescent, or between the body without organs and the organism) remain linear, with a "positive" and a "negative" term, whereas the logic of grace contains a moment of radical passivity and requires a nonlinear rupture that destabilizes the difference between the "positive" and "negative" terms: the sinful are saved and the "righteous" are unsaved.[3] The way in which discriminating judgment and its attendant hierarchies can return at a metalevel in Deleuze's thought (for example, with the good of being beyond good and evil, and the evil of not being beyond good and evil) is undermined by the passive, nonlinear rupture of grace.

Another way of expressing this difference is to say that grace subverts the linear economy of the accumulation of credit and debt just as it ruptures the logic of intention, action, and reward. This means that Nietzsche and Deleuze's characterization of Christianity as a religion of infinite indebtedness does not reflect the biblical witness, because debt requires the linear continuity of accumulated incomings and outgoings. Grace, by contrast, is "a generosity in excess of all calculable economy," and God's gift "remains gift to the end, despite all our efforts to convert it into

---

3. Those who consider themselves righteous in a linear way—that is to say, as a direct and linear consequence of their attitudes and actions—are regularly condemned by Christ and his apostles. See, e.g., Luke 18:9–14; Mark 2:17; Rom. 3:19–24.

debt."[4] It is always possible, along with Deleuze and Nietzsche, to see in the language of grace a veil for debt, but as Hart points out, this reveals more about the prejudice of the one who chooses to read it in that way than it does about biblical grace.

---

4. David Bentley Hart, *The Beauty of the Infinite: The Aesthetics of Christian Truth* (Grand Rapids: Eerdmans, 2004), 372.

9

BECOMING ESCHATOLOGICAL

We now turn to examine biblical eschatology in the light of Deleuze's account of becoming. In *Difference and Repetition,* Deleuze contrasts a Christian sort of repetition, which he sees in Søren Kierkegaard and Charles Péguy, with his own Nietzschean variety. The deficiency of the Christian repetition of resurrection, for Deleuze, is that it is more a one-time recovery of something lost than a continual exploration of new virtualities. It is a restoration rather than a creation, "a self rediscovered and a god recovered" (*DR,* 95) rather than an opening onto anything new. This characterization has some merit: the resurrection (whether we intend Christ's resurrection or the resurrection of the dead at the parousia) is indeed a one-time event and not a constantly renewed and open generation of difference, but Deleuze's account fails to capture the subtleties of the biblical picture of eschatological transformation. Once more, we will find that the biblical account diagonalizes Deleuze's opposition between Platonic eternal stasis and his own ontology of difference.

Transformation, for the Christian, is a past, present, and future reality. First, if anyone is in Christ, he has been transformed with a transformation as radical—and, to use the term we introduced in the previous section, nonlinear—as the creation of the world itself (2 Cor. 5:16–17).[1] Second, in the "last days" between Christ's ascension and return, the Christian is in the process of being constantly transformed "from one degree of glory to another" (3:17–18). Finally, in 1 Corinthians 15:51–53, Paul describes the future transformation awaiting Christians:

> Behold! I tell you a mystery. We shall not all sleep, but we shall all be changed, in a moment, in the twinkling of an eye, at the last trumpet. For the trumpet will sound, and the dead will be raised imperishable, and we shall be changed. For this perishable body must put on the imperishable, and this mortal body must put on immortality.[2]

The Christian's experience is one of transformation in past, present, and future tenses. Furthermore, this transformation takes on ontological significance, for any understanding of "the way things are" currently cannot be adequately articulated without reference to the future parousia when the creation will be transformed. "The way things are" is irreducibly haunted by the reality of the eschaton, a temporal feature of biblical emplotment that Stanley Grenz and John Franke try to capture when they evoke an "eschatological ontology" and an "eschatological realism."[3]

1. "From now on, therefore, we regard no one according to the flesh. Even though we once regarded Christ according to the flesh, we regard him thus no longer. Therefore, if anyone is in Christ, he is a new creation. The old has passed away; behold, the new has come" (2 Cor. 5:16–17).

2. Cf. 1 John 3:2: "Beloved, we are God's children now, and what we will be has not yet appeared; but we know that when he appears we shall be like him, because we shall see him as he is."

3. Stanley J. Grenz and John R. Franke, *Beyond Foundationalism: Shaping Theology in a Postmodern Context* (Louisville, KY: Westminster John Knox Press, 2001), 271. Kevin Vanhoozer engages with the idea and rebaptizes it "theodramatic realism" in "Pilgrim's Digress: Christian Thinking on and about the Post/modern Way," in

Whereas naive realism understands the world that it apprehends in the present to be objective reality, eschatological realism holds that "the objectivity set forth in the biblical narrative is the objectivity of the world as God wills it," and the world as God wills it "lies in the eschatological future," so "the 'actual' universe is the universe as it one day will be," and this future reality "is far more real—and hence far more objective, far more actual—than the present world, which is even now passing away."[4] To apprehend the world objectively is to apprehend with the "eschatological realism" of this forward-looking perspective, to understand the objective reality of things not simply in terms of their current state but in terms of the future realization of their fullness at the eschaton. The temporality of eschatological realism is not captured in Deleuze's characterization of Christian repetition as return, any more than the picture of the new heavens and new earth in Revelation 21 and 22 is simply a recovery of the garden paradise lost in Genesis 3. This eschatological realism sets the reality of transformation, not simply of restoration, at the heart of ontology. There is a certain resonance with Deleuzian ontology here, for in the same way that Grenz and Franke understand objective reality in terms of its to-be-transformed character, Deleuze understands a thing's essence not as what it currently is but as its power to become: "Essence is always difference" (*PS*, 75).

Where Deleuze's essence-as-becoming and eschatological realism differ is in how they understand freedom and constraint in relation to becoming. The difference is not, as Deleuze thinks, in the one-time transformation of Christian repetition, because the resurrection is only one moment in the Christian mythos of transformation. Nothing in Revelation 21–22 suggests that the postresurrection reality of the new heavens and new earth will

Christianity and the Postmodern Turn: Six Views, ed. Myron B. Penner (Grand Rapids: Baker, 2005), 98.

4. Grenz and Franke, *Beyond Foundationalism*, 272.

be a place of stasis, or that once the new Jerusalem comes down from heaven there will be no further transformation. The reality of the new earth is presented in primarily relational terms,[5] and relationships change and develop through time. Though there is no explicit and unambiguous biblical warrant for the position, the new earth has often been understood as a place of development and change, a view pithily captured by C. S. Lewis at the close of *The Last Battle*, the final volume of his Narnia series. As his protagonists contemplate the mountains "higher than you could see in this world" with orchards and waterfalls "going up for ever,"[6] Lewis writes, "Now at last they were beginning Chapter One of the Great Story which no one on earth has read: which goes on for ever: in which every chapter is better than the one before."[7] The parousia is not, on this view, the end of the Christian mythos; it is not the command to "stay where you are" but to "come further up, come further in!"[8] It is neither Platonic stasis nor Deleuze's proliferating becoming, though it is closer to the latter in the following way: in the same way that Deleuzian becoming is free though guided by the desire to maximize potential and is not at liberty to vary from that desire, so also the Christian eschaton is part of an unscripted journey that is about knowing God with increasing intimacy, and is not at liberty to vary from that desire.

---

5. See, e.g., Rev. 21:10–11, 22–23.

6. C. S. Lewis, *The Last Battle* (New York: HarperCollins, 1956), 183.

7. Lewis, *The Last Battle*, 184.

8. "Further Up and Further In" is the title of the fifteenth and penultimate chapter of *The Last Battle*, and the refrain is repeated often in the book.

CONCLUSION

At the end of our discussion of Deleuze and the Bible, we are in a position to discern some repeated patterns that have characterized the conversation. Over the course of the second half of this book, we have drawn a series of comparisons between Deleuze and the Bible, sometimes suggesting that the two are not as polarized as we might be tempted to think. It is important to stress, however, that our approach has been one of comparing the Deleuzian and biblical responses to particular problems, not of comparing Deleuze's assumptions to those of the Bible. If Deleuze and the Bible are close on some matters (or at least closer than Plato is to the Bible), we cannot conclude that they are really saying the same thing in different ways; such a conclusion would respect neither Deleuze nor the Bible. We should not assume that because Deleuze and the Bible start from profoundly different assumptions, they can never offer responses to problems that resemble each other; nor should we assume that because Deleuze and the Bible offer some responses to problems that resemble each other, they must necessarily share the same assumptions. Both of these conclusions would represent a hasty refusal to engage properly with Deleuze and the biblical texts.

If we wish to avoid these two inadequate conclusions, what might we say about the relationship between Deleuze and the Bible? Two things. First of all, we have seen time and again how the Bible draws attention to just how similar the positions of Deleuze and Plato are. This is, of course, no surprise to Deleuze himself, who explicitly states that the overturning of Platonism is not the systematic rejection of all of Plato's categories and assumptions, for "was it not Plato himself who pointed out the direction for the reversal of Platonism?" (*LS*, 256). What is revealed by juxtaposing both Deleuze and Plato to the Bible, however, is that Deleuze's responses to the problems raised in Plato's philosophy are by no means the only responses possible, and indeed it is quite conceivable to challenge Plato in ways not contemplated by Deleuze.

We can therefore usefully characterize the relationship between Deleuze and Plato in terms of the schema employed by Alvin Plantinga to describe the relationship between Christianity and the natural sciences.[1] It might first appear that there are superficial similarities but profound differences between Deleuze and Plato: they share a vocabulary of simulacrum, copies, and truth, for example, but Deleuze understands the place of simulacrum radically differently from Plato. When we bring them both into conversation with the Bible, however, we see that in fact they share superficial differences but profound similarities: they may think of the relationship between truth, identity, and becoming very differently, but this is possible only because of the deeper assumptions they share—for example, the identification of transcendence with a certain kind of metaphysical and political order. At a number of points and in a number of ways, the Bible diagonalizes the assumptions shared by Plato and Deleuze,

---

1. Alvin Plantinga, *Where the Conflict Really Lies: Science, Religion, and Naturalism* (Oxford: Oxford University Press, 2012).

and on occasion we have seen that Deleuze and Plato occupy two positions that each represent only part of a greater reality revealed in the Bible, and can in these instances be understood as Christian heretics.

We have, furthermore, seen the importance of taking a biblical theological approach to a philosopher such as Deleuze, whose interconnected concepts cannot be atomized and abstracted from their context. We have seen that when we try to understand the key moments of biblical emplotment—creation, fall, redemption, and consummation—in relation to each other and as part of an overarching biblical mythos, we discover a Christianity that once more cuts across and rearranges Deleuze's categories. For example, Deleuze's insistence on the primacy of guilt and debt in Christianity isolates the fall from the mythopoetic framework of creation and redemption in the context of which it sits. This framework itself also serves to diagonalize some of the fundamental oppositions on which Deleuze's reading of Plato and his own thought both rely, such as guilt and affirmation or transcendence and immanence.

We must be careful here about the precise nature of this reading of Deleuze. I am not suggesting, in the first instance, that Deleuze ought to have read the Bible more carefully. This would misunderstand what Deleuze is seeking to do when he engages with other philosophers and systems of thought. Deleuze's book on Hume is not an attempt to reconstruct Hume's philosophical system piece by piece, just as Hume would have understood it; his two books on Spinoza are not intended to be faithful mirror images of Spinoza's own thought, nor is his account of the dogmatic image of thought intended to be what Derrida would call a "doubling commentary,"[2] a precise point-by-point recapitulation

2. Jacques Derrida, *Of Grammatology* (Baltimore: Johns Hopkins University Press, 1998), 158–59.

of the source text. Deleuze reads other thinkers in order to help him respond to the problems that he has identified for his own philosophy. He famously describes his encounters with other thinkers as a "taking from behind":

> I myself "did" history of philosophy for a long time, read books on this or that author. But I compensated in various ways . . . . I suppose the main way I coped with it at the time was to see the history of philosophy as a sort of buggery or (if it comes to the same thing) immaculate conception. I imagined myself getting onto the back of an author, and giving him a child, which would be his and which would at the same time be a monster. It is very important that it should be his child, because the author actually had to say everything that I made him say. But it also had to be a monster because it was necessary to go through all kinds of decenterings, slips, break-ins, secret emissions, which I really enjoyed. (*Ne*, 6)

We might want to critique this approach per se, but we should not chastise Deleuze for doing what he said he would do. He engages with the theological tradition not in order to offer a faithful reading of it, but to help him address the problems of freedom, becoming, and transcendence with which his thought engages.

If there is a critique to be made, I think it falls elsewhere: Deleuze's conception of the possibilities open to him in challenging the dogmatic image of thought is too narrow, and it shares much more in common with that image than is necessary. Through identifying Christianity so strongly with the dogmatic image of thought, Deleuze misses resources that would at least help him to refine his own position and at most cause him to rethink his dismissal of Christianity. His overturning of Platonism lacks the radical incisiveness and the nonlinear rupture of the critique of Platonism offered by a biblical theological approach such as we have begun to sketch in these pages, for it challenges Plato's content while aping and affirming many of his gestures. Deleuze overturns Platonism, but biblical theology overturns, in a more radical gesture, the twins Plato and Deleuze.

GLOSSARY

Deleuze's vocabulary is richer than it is possible to capture in this brief glossary. Entries below refer to terms referenced in this volume. For a more comprehensive glossary of Deleuzian terms, see Adrian Paar, ed., *The Deleuze Dictionary*. Terms with entries in the glossary are in bold.

abstract machine. See *machine.*

actual. See *virtual and actual.*

arborescence. In *A Thousand Plateaus*, a structure's obedience to a hierarchical order, with a single controlling concept (such as God) to which all other elements are subordinated. The arborescent schema is a closed, static, and stable structure. Arborescence resembles Porphyry's tree. See also *nomadism; rhizome.*

becoming (becoming-woman, becoming-animal, becoming-plant, becoming-imperceptible). A feature of Deleuze's ontology that is, in contrast to the Platonic Western ontology of identity and being, one of becoming and difference. Becoming for Deleuze is not subordinated to being as the transition between two stable states, but rather being itself is nothing but a very slow becoming. In *A Thousand Plateaus*, Deleuze and Guattari introduce a series of becomings: *becoming-woman* is a disruption of norms because there is no fixed standard in the Western tradition for what a woman should be; *becoming-animal* is a way of seeking to understand how an animal perceives and understands the world that prevents us from seeing our modes of perception as fixed and unchangeable; and *becoming-imperceptible* is a term with many meanings (*ATP*, 308), including cultivating a mode of perception that goes beyond the perception of different beings to apprehend the microscopic differences that we usually miss.

Bergson, Henri (1859–1941). French philosopher whose account of time deeply influenced Deleuze in the 1960s. In *Matter and Memory*, Bergson thinks of time not in terms of extension but as duration (*durée*), in which present apprehension and past memory are inextricable from each other. Bergson also introduces the virtual/actual distinction, which Deleuze develops in *Bergsonism* and *Difference and Repetition*. See also *virtual and actual*.

Bergsonism **(1966/1988).** A work in which Deleuze develops and articulates his own reading of Bergson's philosophy, including his concepts of duration, memory, and the virtual. Deleuze sees Bergsonian duration (*durée*) as giving us a notion of time that breaks with the linear model common in Western thought. The book is important not only as a major reading of Bergson but as an explanation of some of the key concepts in Deleuze's own thought. See also *linear and nonlinear thought*; *virtual and actual*.

body without organs (BwO). A nonorganized or noncentralized body that resists hierarchical structure. The term is taken from Antonin Artaud and used in *The Logic of Sense*,

Anti-Oedipus, and *A Thousand Plateaus*. The body without organs (often abbreviated by Deleuze and Guattari to *BwO*, in French *CsO*) "is opposed not to the organs but to that organization of the organs called the organism" (*ATP*, 158). The BwO is not a subject closed in on itself but is open to new machinic assemblages. See also *machine; organism; rhizome*.

conatus. The effort to persevere in being. The term was used by Spinoza.

crowned anarchies. Nonhierarchical distributions of entities (*DR*, 278, 304) that contrast with Plato's hierarchical ordering of ideas and copies. The term was borrowed from Antonin Artaud and used by Deleuze in *Difference and Repetition*, *The Logic of Sense*, and *A Thousand Plateaus*. Also termed *nomadic distribution*. See also *nomadism*.

desire. A key term for Deleuze and Guattari in *Anti-Oedipus* and *A Thousand Plateaus*. Whereas for psychoanalysis desire connotes lack and absence and is governed by the Oedipal law of desiring the mother and seeking to kill the father, Deleuze's notion of desire is not for something that is lacking, and it is not constrained by an overarching law. Desire is positive and productive of life, forging connections and increasing the power of bodies. See also *desiring-machine; desiring-production*.

desiring-machine. In *Anti-Oedipus*, any series of connections through which desire flows, as in the example of a newborn hand and mouth, and a breast. These desiring-machines are operative before there is any sense of a "mother" or a "baby": it is a desiring-machine that seeks the comfort of the breast, not an organism. See also *desiring-production; machine*.

desiring-production. A key concept in *Anti-Oedipus* that brings together Freud (desire) and Marx (production) to describe the "universal primary process" that undergirds nature, society, and the mind. Desiring-production is, like Spinoza's conatus or Nietzsche's will to power, a force that animates the world and makes reality. Desire is productive for Deleuze and Guattari because it is a positive, creative force and not an absence or a lack as it is in psychoanalysis. See also *desiring-machine*.

difference. A term fundamental to Deleuze's philosophy, in which context it means not difference between two or more stable forms ("A is different from B"), but a "difference-in-itself" that is original and not subordinated to identity. For the dogmatic image of thought, "only that which resembles differs" (*LS*, 261), but in Deleuze's own account, "only differences can resemble each other" (*LS*, 261). See also *extensive/intensive; multiplicity*.

dogmatic image of thought. The outlook that, according to Deleuze, has dominated the West in various forms since Plato, and that is characterized by its assumption that truth is both desired and attainable, that error does not belong to thought itself, and that thinking well is accomplished by employing a method that wards off error. An *image of thought* is an "implicit, subjective, and preconceptual" (*WIP*, 61) set of assumptions that "determines our goals when we try to think" (*DR*, xvi), and that gives us a reason to think in the first place. Deleuze does not replace the dogmatic image of thought with another image that he considers preferable, but seeks "a liberation of thought from those images which imprison it" (*DR*, xvii). The term is discussed at length in the third chapter of *Difference and Repetition*. See also *difference; icon; recognition; representation; simulacrum; subject; transcendence*.

duration (*durée*). See *Bergson*.

empiricism. See *transcendental empiricism*.

eschatological realism. A term used by Stanley Grenz and John Franke to describe the way in which, for the Christian, "the 'actual' universe is the universe as it one day will be," and this future reality "is far more real—and hence far more objective, far more actual—than the present world, which is even now passing away."[1] That which is most real is not our immediate experience, and neither is it a Platonic world of Forms; it is the reality of the new creation.

eternal return. A concept found in Nietzsche's *The Gay Science* in which all events recur repeatedly over an infinite span of time, lending weight to our actions in the present without the need for a God who judges them. Deleuze's appropriation of the idea is distinctively his own: "every time we interpret the eternal return as the return of the identical or the same, we replace Nietzsche's thought with childish hypotheses" (*NaP*, xi), for what in fact returns is the virtual difference and becoming from which past events were actualized, not the actualized identities themselves. See also *virtual and actual.*

extensive/intensive. An opposition that describes two ways of understanding the world. The extensive thinks of the world spatially, in terms of Cartesian coordinates in which all objects can be plotted in relation to one another across larger or smaller distances. The extensive is often contrasted to intensities, which are not objects but qualities that are in constant becoming, waxing or waning in intensity. Time for Deleuze is intensive, following different durations for different organisms. In the same way that Deleuze's reversal of Platonism sets difference at the origin of identity, he insists that extension is a product of intensity:

---

1. Stanley J. Grenz and John R. Franke, *Beyond Foundationalism: Shaping Theology in a Postmodern Context* (Louisville, KY: Westminster John Knox Press, 2001), 272.

forces produce objects, not the other way around. The
opposition between the intensive and the extensive runs
through Deleuze's thought from *Difference and Repetition*
to *A Thousand Plateaus*.

Freud, Sigmund (1856–1939). The founder of psychoanalysis
whose account of desire as lack and the familial Oedipal
triangle is attacked in Deleuze and Guattari's *Anti-Oedipus*.

Guattari, Félix (1930–92). Deleuze's coauthor on the two volumes of *Capitalism and Schizophrenia*, *Kafka: Toward a Minor
Literature*, and *What Is Philosophy?* Their working relationship has been characterized in terms of their famous account
of the wasp and the orchid from *A Thousand Plateaus*: "Wasp
and orchid, as heterogeneous elements, form a rhizome"
constituting "a veritable becoming, a becoming-wasp of the
orchid and a becoming-orchid of the wasp" (*ATP*, 10).

icon. In Plato's theory of Forms, a "good copy" or a faithful
though imperfect reproduction of an eternal Form. Plato
gives the example of a bed made by a carpenter that,
because it is indeed a bed, participates in the eternal Form
of the bed. See also *dogmatic image of thought*; *simulacrum*.

image of thought. See *dogmatic image of thought*.

immanence. See *plane of immanence*.

intensive. See *extensive/intensive*.

judgment of God. A term borrowed and adapted from Antonin
Artaud to characterize God in terms of order, stability, and
hierarchy: "the judgment of God is nothing other than the
power to organize to infinity" (*ECC*, 130). The judgment
of God is conservative and reactionary because it "presupposes pre-existing criteria" and so "can neither apprehend
what is new in an existing being nor even sense the creation
of a mode of existence" (*ECC*, 134–35).

Kant, Immanuel (1724–1804). A major antagonist of Deleuze,
though they also share some elements of methodology.

Difference and Repetition has been understood as a response to, and rewriting of, Kant's *Critique of Pure Reason*. Both Kant and Deleuze undertake transcendental investigations, seeking conditions of possibility, but whereas Kant searches for the conditions of possible experience, Deleuze is concerned for the origin of real experience; and whereas Kant traces the origin of the world of appearance to noumenal realities, for Deleuze it is difference that is at the origin of all existence.

linear and nonlinear thought. A distinction used in the present volume to contrast both Plato and Deleuze with a Reformed doctrine of grace. Both Plato and Deleuze distinguish between one sort of entity or event that is positively valued (the "true" copies of Platonic Forms for Plato or the becoming of simulacra for Deleuze) and a second sort that is negatively valued ("false" simulacra for Plato or the so-called "true" copies that Deleuze denounces). By contrast, grace is nonlinear insofar as it requires a rupture of the linear sequence of intentions and actions with an intervention from outside, and it detaches or uncouples the will from its self-chosen orientation.

machine. An assemblage of parts in which the focus is on the interaction of individual elements rather than the overall purpose or integrity of the whole, and on action rather than meaning: a machine does something, rather than simply meaning something. *Machine* is an important term for Deleuze and Guattari in *Anti-Oedipus* and *A Thousand Plateaus*, but it is almost always part of a compound noun such as *desiring-machine, war machine*, and *abstract machine*. The organization of the body without organs is machinic because it is not centralized and has no fixed boundaries.

majoritarian/minoritarian. A distinction used by Deleuze and Guattari to describe the characteristics of dominant and subordinate positions. In *Kafka: Toward a Minor Literature*, Deleuze and Guattari define a "minor" literature as one that deterritorializes language, destabilizing conventional grammar, rhythms, and stresses, and one that stresses social and political concerns. The categories of the majoritarian and minoritarian in *A Thousand Plateaus* further develop this idea: the majoritarian is that which provides a stable norm (for example, "the average adult white-heterosexual European-male speaking a standard language" [*ATP*, 105]); a minoritarian group, by contrast, has no fixed identity but is in a process of becoming.

minoritarian. See *majoritarian/minoritarian*.

minor literature. See *majoritarian/minoritarian*.

multiplicity. A term that Deleuze adapted from Bergson to describe a field of pure difference. Like *difference, multiplicity* is a key Deleuzian term, and like *difference*, it is not a multiplicity *of* anything but "a pure multiplicity in the Idea which radically excludes the identical as a prior condition" (*DR*, 211–12). Multiplicity is originary, and identities emerge only when multiplicities slow down.

Nietzsche, Friedrich (1844–1900). Nineteenth-century German philosopher whose concepts of the will to power and eternal return are instrumental in the development of Deleuze's own thought and on whom Deleuze wrote two books: *Nietzsche and Philosophy* (1962/1983) and *Nietzsche* (1965, trans. in *Pure Immanence*, 2001).

nomadic. Of or relating to a group that has its principle of organization within itself, not imposed from above. A nomadic politics, then, is a politics that does not impose rigid order from above but allows fluid arborescent relations to emerge from below. The term is used in *Anti-Oedipus* and *A Thousand Plateaus*. See also *arborescence; crowned anarchies*.

organism. In *A Thousand Plateaus* and elsewhere, a body with a centralized structure and organs arranged in strict hierarchy. An organism is the bodily equivalent of Plato's distinction between Form and copy, with the primacy of identity over difference and being over becoming. See also *body without organs.*

overturning of Platonism. See *reversal of Platonism.*

parousia. In theology, the "appearing" of Christ when he returns to judge the world.

plane of immanence. A concept that describes reality in a way that excludes any appeal to transcendence. The plane of immanence contains all the principles and assumptions, all the concepts and relationships, that govern our thought and action. It is a *plane* of immanence because there are no hierarchies in being—no instance of difference has more or less being than any other—and it is a plane of *immanence* because there is no transcendent God or substance to organize the differentiating and becoming of everything that is. The plane of immanence is a key notion in Deleuze's philosophy of immanence, which refuses any transcendent norms, such as moral laws, or transcendent beings, such as God. The term is used in *A Thousand Plateaus* and *What Is Philosophy?* Also termed *plane of consistency.* See also *Spinoza.*

Porphyry's tree. A schema classifying all living things on a scale of being in relation to a sequence of criteria designating what they have in common. Named after the third-century B.C. Greek Neoplatonist philosopher Porphyry, *Porphyry's tree* is used by Deleuze as an instance of the primacy of identity over difference. Also termed *Porphyrian tree.* See also *arborescence.*

recognition. The aspect of the dogmatic image of thought that seeks to match things in the world to preexisting eternal

Forms. For the paradigm of recognition, to know the truth of something is to recognize its correspondence to a Form. See also *representation*.

representation. The aspect of the dogmatic image of thought that understands thinking to be a mirroring of the world. It operates according to rigid criteria and is unable to take account of difference in itself. See also *recognition*.

reversal of Platonism. Deleuze's mode of engaging with the principles of the dogmatic image of thought as they are formulated in Plato's philosophy. In *The Logic of Sense*, the reversal of Platonism is understood not as the reversal of original and copy, of Form and icon, but as a disruption of Plato's hierarchy between icon and simulacrum. "In the reversal of Platonism, resemblance is said of internalized difference, and identity of the Different as primary power" (*LS*, 262): whereas for Plato identity precedes and grounds difference, in the reversal of Platonism identity is a product of the suppression of an originary difference. Deleuze stresses that this is not a simple rejection of Plato's thought, for "was it not Plato himself who pointed out the direction for the reversal of Platonism?" (*LS*, 256). Also termed *overturning of Platonism*. See also *extensive/intensive*.

rhizome. A botanical term for a type of plant comprising a stem or root system that is not hierarchically organized and has no center or trunk, only nodes, roots, and shoots. In *A Thousand Plateaus*, Deleuze and Guattari contrast hierarchical, rigid arborescent structures with the nonhierarchical, noncentralized rhizome. The body without organs is structured as a rhizome, and Deleuze and Guattari wrote *A Thousand Plateaus* itself as a "rhizome-book." See also *arborescence*.

scandal of the historical. One of the three scandals that characterize the incarnation in the Bible. In Christ, the eternal, unchanging God is irreducibly historical: Christ is not an abstract eternal reality but has a particular human genealogy, being "descended from David according to the flesh" (Rom. 1:3). It is a scandal to some systems of thought, Platonism being one of them, that ultimate reality could ever be present in history in this way. See also *scandal of the material; scandal of the particular.*

scandal of the material. One of the three scandals that characterize the incarnation in the Bible. The claim in the prologue to John's Gospel that "the Word became flesh" (John 1:14) is a scandal for those who labor under the Platonic or Enlightenment prejudice that ultimate reality must be pure, abstract, and universal. The incarnation is not just a scandal of the material in the sense that Christ had a physical body, however, for it vindicates and dignifies the material world as such. In the present volume, it is argued that this Christian vindication of materiality stands in contrast to both Plato and Deleuze. See also *scandal of the historical; scandal of the particular.*

scandal of the particular. One of the three scandals that characterize the incarnation in the Bible. God was incarnate not as an abstract human being but as a particular first-century Palestinian Aramaic-speaking male Jew: Jesus of Nazareth. Along with the scandal of the historical and the scandal of the material, this particularity offends an Enlightenment sensibility for which truth is understood to be impersonal and abstract. Christ is not the ideal embodiment of an abstract idea that transcends him; his universality is not deeper than his particularity. The present volume argues that this scandal of the particular stands in contrast to both Platonic transcendence and the Deleuzian virtual. See also *virtual and actual.*

schizoanalysis. A term in *Anti-Oedipus* in opposition to Freudian psychoanalysis. Whereas psychoanalysis models the psyche on neurosis, schizoanalysis models it on schizophrenia. Whereas psychoanalysis conceives desire as lack and traps it in the Oedipal triangle, schizoanalysis widens the field of investigation beyond the psychological to fragments or "schizzes" incorporating economic forces of "social pro- duction" alongside psychic forces of desiring-production, and seeks to free people from the oppression of desire in psychoanalysis.

simulacrum. In Plato's theory of Forms, a "bad copy" that does not participate in an eternal Form. Plato gives the example of an artist's depiction of a bed, which is a false copy because it is not itself a bed. The notion of simulacrum more or less disappeared from Deleuze's work after the publication of *Difference and Repetition* and *The Logic of Sense*. See also *dogmatic image of thought; icon*.

Spinoza, Baruch (1632–77). Hailed by Deleuze and Guattari as the "Christ of philosophers" (*WIP*, 60) in comparison to whom "the greatest philosophers are hardly more than apostles who distance themselves or draw near this mys- tery" (*WIP*, 60). Spinoza's radical notions of the univocity of being, conatus, and substance and modes shape Deleuze's understanding of immanence. See also *plane of immanence*.

subject, the. A term used in relation to the philosophy of Descartes to describe a unified, self-conscious, rationally governed self. The subject is the self who can say, "I think, therefore I am," with the *I* who thinks being identical to the *I* who is. For Deleuze, the subject is a figure at home in the dogmatic image of thought.

transcendence. A characteristic of the dogmatic image of thought that locates the truth in a realm beyond experience. Deleuze condemns this dualism in the strongest terms: "The poisoned gift of Platonism is to have introduced tran- scendence into philosophy, to have given transcendence a plausible philosophical meaning" (*ECC*, 137). For Deleuze, a belief in transcendence leads to nihilism when confidence in the existence of the higher world is lost. See also *plane of immanence*; *transcendental, the.*

transcendental, the. A term describing an inquiry after the conditions necessary for a given phenomenon or experience. For example, in the *Critique of Pure Reason*, Kant undertakes a transcendental investigation into the necessary conditions of possible experience. In *Difference and Repetition*, Deleuze frames his own philosophy as transcendental, but in contrast to Kant, he is seeking the origin of real experience. Not to be confused with transcendence. See also *transcendental empiricism.*

transcendental empiricism. In *Difference and Repetition*, Deleuze's term to describe both the thought of Antonin Artaud and his own philosophical method. This seemingly paradoxical combination of transcendental (Kant) and empirical (Hume) approaches is reconciled by Deleuze in the following way: his method is transcendental because it seeks to discover the necessary conditions of experience (hence transcendental), and it is empirical because it infers those conditions from experience itself (hence empiricist). The great wager of Deleuze's method is that the transcendental and the empirical are not the incommensurable approaches that they have often been assumed to be.

univocity of being. In Spinoza's philosophy, the position that *being* always means the same thing, no matter whether we are talking about God, minds, bodies, ideas, or rocks. In Deleuze's terms, "a single voice raises the clamor of being" (*DR*, 35).

virtual and actual. A distinction that Deleuze borrows from Bergson, for whom it is opposed to the possible and the real. Whereas possibility is less than reality, the real minus existence, the virtual is just as real as the actual, and together they form the two "dissimilar halves" of reality (*DR*, 209–10). The difference between virtual and actual is that while the virtual is pure becoming and variation of multiplicity, the actual tends to pure identity.

will to power. A term used by Nietzsche but never truly defined by him, indicating the fundamental motivation or desire of all human action. In a section of *Nietzsche and Philosophy* entitled "What Is the Will to Power?," Deleuze insists that it is a force that cannot be reduced to the will of any subject; it is being itself that wills power.

SELECT BIBLIOGRAPHY
AND REFERENCES

Works by Deleuze[1]

(1953) *Empirisme et subjectivité*. Paris: PUF. Translated as *Empiricism and Subjectivity*, by Constantin Boundas. New York: Columbia University Press, 1991. Deleuze's first book, exploring the philosophy of David Hume. As with all of Deleuze's other readings of major thinkers, his reconstruction of Hume's philosophy is distinctive and serves his own philosophical ends. For Deleuze, Hume's major concern is with the place of subjectivity within nature, and his response is: "We are habits, nothing but habits—the habit of saying 'I'" (*ES*, x).

(1962) *Nietzsche et la philosophie*. Paris: PUF. Translated as *Nietzsche and Philosophy*, by Hugh Tomlinson. Minneapolis: University of Minnesota Press, 1983. The first of two books by Deleuze on Nietzsche written in the 1960s. Deleuze explores and argues for new interpretations of the Nietzschean ideas of the will to power and eternal return, ideas and interpretations that will exert a continual influence on his own later thought.

---

1. Texts coauthored with Félix Guattari are prefixed with an asterisk (*).

(1963) *La Philosophie critique de Kant*. Paris: PUF. Translated as *The Critical Philosophy of Kant*, by Hugh Tomlinson and Barbara Habberjam. Minneapolis: University of Minnesota Press, 1984. This key early engagement with Kant situates him as both Deleuze's antagonist and his ally. Deleuze commends Kant for seeking a purely *immanent* critique of reason in terms not of errors external to reason but of its internal illusions, but argues that Kant failed to find what he sought. He also shares Kant's transcendental approach, but whereas the Kant of the *Critique of Pure Reason* has recourse to the noumenon as the condition of possibility of experience, Deleuze locates pure difference at the origin of being.

(1964 [1970, 1976]) *Proust et les signes*. Paris: PUF. 1976 ed. translated as *Proust and Signs: The Complete Text*, by Richard Howard. Minneapolis: University of Minnesota Press, 2003. Deleuze traces through Proust's multivolume novel *Remembrance of Things Past* a network of signs, showing how the perception of Albertine, the narrator's beloved, opens up another world. This reading allows Deleuze to frame the literary text as a machine for the production of signs. The text was republished in 1970 and again in 1976, the final edition being twice the size of the first and showing the influence of Guattari on Deleuze's thought.

(1965) *Nietzsche*. Paris: PUF. Translated in *Pure Immanence*.

(1966) *Le Bergsonisme*. Paris: PUF. Translated as *Bergsonism*, by Hugh Tomlinson and Barbara Habberjam. New York: Zone Books, 1988.

(1967) *Présentation de Sacher-Masoch*. Paris: Minuit. Translated as *Masochism: An Interpretation of Coldness and Cruelty*, by Jean McNeil. New York: G. Braziller, 1971.

(1968) *Différence et répétition*. Paris: PUF. Translated as *Difference and Repetition*, by Paul Patton. New York: Columbia University Press, 1994. Deleuze's first magnum opus, in which he sets the course for his future thought. Deleuze rejects representation and the dogmatic image of thought in favor of a transcendental empiricism as he constructs his philosophy of *difference in itself* and *repetition for itself*—that is to say, difference and repetition that are not contingent on any prior sameness or identity. Building on Nietzsche's notion of eternal return, Deleuze argues that what is repeated is nothing other than difference itself.

(1968) *Spinoza et le problème de l'expression*. Paris: Minuit. Translated as *Expressionism in Philosophy: Spinoza*, by Martin Joughin. New York: Zone Books, 1990. The first of two major works by Deleuze on Spinoza. *Expressionism in Philosophy: Spinoza* was Deleuze's minor doctoral thesis, *Difference and Repetition* being its major counterpart. Deleuze explores Spinoza's univocity of being and his position that all beings are modal expressions of a single substance. Unusually, Deleuze's reading of Spinoza here seems to be an attempt at a faithful reconstruction of Spinoza's thought rather than a means of exploring Deleuze's own thinking.

(1969) *Logique du sens*. Paris: Minuit. Translated as *The Logic of Sense*, by Mark Lester with Charles Stivale. New York: Columbia University Press, 1990. Along with *Difference and Repetition*, *The Logic of Sense* is the second Deleuzian magnum opus to predate his collaboration with Félix Guattari. Deleuze seeks to account for the origin of sense, which is a prerequisite for truth (if a proposition has no sense, it is neither true nor false). The appendix "Simulacrum and Ancient Philosophy" sets out Deleuze's ontology and his reversal of Platonism and leads on to a discussion of the simulacrum in the work of the ancient atomist philosopher Lucretius.

(1970) *Spinoza: Philosophie pratique*. Paris: Editions du Minuit. Translated as *Spinoza: Practical Philosophy*, by Robert Hurley. San Francisco: City Lights Books, 1988. The second of two major works by Deleuze on Spinoza, this book discusses Spinoza's philosophy in conversation with Nietzsche's *Genealogy of Morals*, discussing at length the difference between ethics and morality. Deleuze also presents Spinoza's main ideas in dictionary form.

*(1972) *Capitalisme et schizophrénie 1. L'Anti-Oedipe*. Paris: Minuit. Translated as *Anti-Oedipus*, by Robert Hurley, Mark Seem, and Helen R. Lane. New York: Viking, 1977. Reprint, Minneapolis:

University of Minnesota Press, 1983. The first of two volumes by Deleuze and Guattari, together known as *Capitalism and Schizophrenia*. The book develops the idea of the body without organs first introduced in *Logic of Sense*, along with important concepts such as the rhizome, desiring-production and desiring-machine, and deterritorialization. The authors reject Freud's theory of repression and his focus on the family as being reactive, idealistic, and slavish, replacing Freudian psychoanalysis with their own schizoanalysis and a positive, productive account of desire.

(1972) Coauthored with Michel Foucault. "*Entretien: les intellectuels et le pouvoir.*" *L'Arc* 49:3–10. Translated as "Intellectuals and Power." In *Language, Counter-Memory, Practice: Selected Essays and Interviews by Michel Foucault*, edited by Donald F. Bouchard, 205–17. Ithaca, NY: Cornell University Press, 1977. A seminal conversation between Deleuze and Foucault in which they discuss the relationship between theory and praxis, and how intellectuals should use their place in society to confront power and help those under oppression.

*(1975) *Kafka: Pour une littérature mineure*. Paris: Minuit. Translated as *Kafka: Toward a Minor Literature*, by Dana Polan. Minneapolis: University of Minnesota Press, 1986. Deleuze and Guattari argue that Kafka's texts are "minor" in the sense that they seek neither to copy established models nor to represent humanity as a whole. It is creative, challenging tradition rather than reproducing it. In a break with prevailing critical opinion, Kafka is presented as a comic and positive writer.

(1977) *Dialogues (avec Claire Parnet)*. Paris: Flammarion. Translated as *Dialogues*, by Hugh Tomlinson and Barbara Habberjam. New York: Columbia University Press, 1987.

*(1980) *Capitalisme et Schizophrénie 2. Mille plateaux*. Paris: Minuit. Translated as *A Thousand Plateaus*, by Brian Massumi. Minneapolis: University of Minnesota Press, 1987. The second of two volumes by Deleuze and Guattari, together known as *Capitalism and Schizophrenia*. The authors describe the text as "a little machine" and a "body without organs" (*ATP*, 4); it

is written as a series of fifteen plateaus (or sections) that are intended to be read in any order. As such, like a rhizome the text has no beginning, middle, or end. *A Thousand Plateaus* discusses important concepts such as becoming, lines of flight, the judgment of God, majoritarian/minoritarian and nomadic/sedentary oppositions, the plane of immanence, and war machines.

(1981) *Francis Bacon: Logique de la sensation.* Paris: Editions de la Différence. Translated as *Francis Bacon: The Logic of Sensation*, by Daniel W. Smith. Minneapolis: University of Minnesota Press, 2005. Deleuze's only book-length piece on a visual artist. Deleuze explores the transcendental realm of the sensation and invents a series of concepts in terms of which the "sensible aggregates" of Bacon's work can be understood. On Deleuze's account, Bacon paints "figures," or "the sensible form related to a sensation" that "acts immediately upon the nervous system" (*FBLS*, 34) through intensities rather than extension, in opposition to the theory of graphic representation.

(1983) *Cinéma 1: L'Image-Mouvement.* Paris: Minuit. Translated as *Cinema 1: The Movement-Image*, by Hugh Tomlinson and Barbara Habberjam. Minneapolis: University of Minnesota Press, 1986.

(1985) *Cinéma 2: l'Image-temps.* Paris: Minuit. Translated as *Cinema 2: The Time-Image*, by Hugh Tomlinson and Barbara Habberjam, Minneapolis: University of Minnesota Press, 1989.

(1986) *Foucault.* Paris: Minuit. Translated as *Foucault*, by Sean Hand. Minneapolis: University of Minnesota Press, 1988. Deleuze and Foucault maintained a deep intellectual friendship, Foucault famously remarking, "Perhaps one day this century will be known as Deleuzian." They split in 1977 over the relation between philosophical thought and its historical context, but Deleuze's interest in Foucault's thought remained. After Foucault's death in 1984, Deleuze wrote his *Foucault*, a book that characteristically thinks with Foucault rather than explaining his work, presenting Foucault as a philosopher of topology or "thinking otherwise."

(1988) *Le Pli: Leibniz et le Baroque.* Paris: Minuit. Translated as *The Fold: Leibniz and the Baroque*, by Tom Conley. Minneapolis:

University of Minnesota Press, 1993. Deleuze uses Leibniz's thought to understand the Baroque period, and reciprocally shines light on Leibniz through considerations of Baroque art, architecture, and music. Deleuze brings them together by reading them both in terms of his own concept of the fold. A Leibnizian monad is not an atom but a fold in time and space, and the world is a series of multiple folds and surfaces. Indeed, "[t]he unit of matter, the smallest element of the labyrinth, is the fold" (*FLB*, 6).

*(1991) *Qu'est-ce que la philosophie?* Paris: Minuit. Translated as *What Is Philosophy?*, by Hugh Tomlinson and Graham Burchell. New York: Columbia University Press, 1994. Deleuze's last cowritten book with Félix Guattari. Their answer to the titular question is that philosophy is the invention of concepts. Philosophy invents concepts on a plane of immanence, science creates functions on a plane of reference, and art creates sensations composed of percepts and affects (*WIP*, 164).

(1993) *Critique et Clinique.* Paris: Minuit. Translated as *Essays Critical and Clinical*, by Daniel Smith and Michael Greco. Minneapolis: University of Minnesota Press, 1997.

(1995) "L'immanence: une vie." *Philosophie* 47 (Septembre 1): 3–7. Translated as "Immanence: A Life." In *Two Regimes of Madness.* New York: Semiotexte, 2006.

(1997) *Negotiations, 1972–1990.* Translated by Martin Joughin. New York: Columbia University Press. A collection of Deleuze's essays and articles, some cowritten with Félix Guattari, with sections on *Anti-Oedipus* and *A Thousand Plateaus*, cinema, Michel Foucault, philosophy, and politics. The self-contained structure of each intervention and the range of topics covered make this one of the best firsthand introductions to Deleuze's thought.

(2001) *Pure Immanence: Essays on a Life.* Edited by John Rajchman. Translated by Anne Boymen. New York: Zone Books.

(2002) *L'Île déserte et autres textes: textes et entretiens 1953–1974.* Edited by David Lapoujade. Paris: Minuit. Translated as *Desert Islands and Other Texts (1953–1974)*, by Mike Taormina. New York: Semiotexte, 2003.

(2003) *Deux régimes de fous: textes et entretiens 1975–1995*. Edited by David Lapoujade. Paris: Minuit. Translated as *Two Regimes of Madness: Texts and Interviews 1975–1995*. New York: Semiotexte, 2006.

Secondary Material on Deleuze

Badiou, Alain. *Deleuze: The Clamor of Being*. Minneapolis: University of Minnesota Press, 2000. Badiou argues that Deleuze is a theologian of transcendence *malgré lui*. Focusing on Deleuze's distinction between the virtual, which he identifies with unity, and the actual, which he identifies with multiplicity, Badiou identifies in Deleuze a privilege of virtual-unity over actual-multiplicity in just the same way that Neoplatonist Christianity privileges God's pure unity over creation's multiplicity. Badiou's reading of Deleuze has been resisted and rebutted by not a few Deleuze scholars,[2] but it remains one of the most important arguments that Deleuze's thought is covertly theological.

Bogue, Ronald. *Deleuze and Guattari*. London: Routledge, 1989.

Bryden, Mary, ed. *Deleuze and Religion*. London: Routledge, 2001. A collection of essays by eminent Deleuze scholars treating the book's subject from a range of perspectives.

Colebrook, Claire. *Gilles Deleuze*. Routledge Critical Thinkers. London: Routledge, 2001.

———. *Understanding Deleuze*. Sydney: Allen and Unwin, 2003.

Crockett, Clayton. *A Theology of the Sublime*. London: Routledge, 2002. Crockett contends that Deleuze can be used to help shape a new "secular" or "radical" theology. Freeing inquiry from the dogma that limits and stifles theological novelty, this approach sees the

---

2. Henry Somers-Hall, "Deleuze's Philosophical Heritage," in *The Cambridge Companion to Deleuze*, ed. Daniel W. Smith and Henry Somers-Hall (Cambridge: Cambridge University Press, 2012), 352; Daniel W. Smith, "The Doctrine of Univocity," in *Deleuze and Religion*, ed. Mary Bryden (London: Routledge, 2001), 174; 181n19; Kristien Justaert, *Theology after Deleuze* (London: Continuum, 2012), 45.

emergence of a new Deleuzian liberation theology,[3] a vision of a world without hierarchies and in which "God" is to be understood, in terms of Deleuze's virtual/actual distinction, as "the virtual *potentia* that makes it possible to restore belief"[4] and "the capacity of immanence to produce beyond all limits of propriety."[5]

Foucault, Michel. "Theatrum Philosophicum." In *Aesthetics, Method, and Epistemology*, edited by James D. Faubion, 343–68. Translated by R. Hurley et al. *Essential Works of Foucault 1954–84*, 2. New York: New Press, 1998. Foucault's extended review of *Difference and Repetition* and *The Logic of Sense*.

Goodchild, Philip. *Deleuze and Guattari: An Introduction to the Politics of Desire*. London: Sage, 1996.

Hallward, Peter. *Out of This World: Deleuze and the Philosophy of Creation*. New York: Verso, 2006. Hallward follows a Badiouian line in interpreting Deleuze, arguing that Deleuze's ethics and politics preach a salvation from the constraints of this world toward the boundless freedom of the virtual. As long as Deleuze's thought retains a notion of the virtual-One, it can never be free of theological influence.

Hart, David Bentley. *The Beauty of the Infinite: The Aesthetics of Christian Truth*. Grand Rapids: Eerdmans, 2004. Hart is an Orthodox theologian whose thesis in *The Beauty of the Infinite* is that "modern Continental philosophy is very much the misbegotten child of theology, indeed a kind of secularized theology,"[6] and he sees a tension between a "Dionysian" moment in Deleuze's thought that affirms this world and an "Apollonian," gnostic moment that seeks to flee the determinacy of this world

---

3. Judith Poxon, "Embodied Anti-theology," in Bryden, *Deleuze and Religion*, 50.

4. Christopher Ben Simpson, *Deleuze and Theology* (London: Bloomsbury, 2012), 101.

5. Anthony Paul Smith and Daniel Whistler, eds., *After the Postsecular and the Postmodern: New Essays in Continental Philosophy of Religion* (Newcastle upon Tyne: Cambridge Scholars Publishing, 2010), 169, quoted in Simpson, *Deleuze and Theology*, 78.

6. David Bentley Hart, *The Beauty of the Infinite: The Aesthetics of Christian Truth* (Grand Rapids: Eerdmans, 2004), 30.

for a purer, virtual existence. He takes a similar line to Badiou, Hallward, and Žižek in arguing that there is something theological in Deleuze's distinction between the actual and the virtual.

Justaert, Kristien. *Theology after Deleuze*. London: Continuum, 2012. Justaert claims that Deleuzian themes can be found in theology—that Deleuze's becoming-imperceptible, for example, helps us to understand the Christian's imitation of Christ. Deleuze enables us to see further into Christian realities, and to apprehend aspects of the faith that would remain hidden were it not for the light that Deleuze's thought shines on the Christian tradition. This all relies, however, on Justaert's claim that philosophy and theology are contemplating the same reality, each with its own vocabulary.[7] The problem with this claim is that it underplays the qualitative difference made by revelation.

May, Todd. *Gilles Deleuze: An Introduction*. Cambridge: Cambridge University Press, 2005.

Milbank, John. *Theology and Social Theory*. Oxford: Blackwell, 2008. Milbank paints with a broad brush, including Deleuze along with other "Continental" thinkers such as Nietzsche, Derrida, and Foucault as participants in what he sees as a nominalist heresy. They reduce difference to "the 'original' and continuous variation of a primordial 'unity.'"[8]

O'Regan, Cyril. *Gnostic Return in Modernity*. Albany: SUNY Press, 2001. O'Regan argues that Deleuze takes aim at a false, Gnostic view of Christianity, and that his God conforms to all six elements of the Valentinian narrative grammar that describe Gnosticism.

Parr, Adrian, ed. *The Deleuze Dictionary: Revised Edition*. Edinburgh: Edinburgh University Press, 2010.

Shults, F. LeRon. *Iconoclastic Theology: Gilles Deleuze and the Secretion of Atheism*. Edinburgh: Edinburgh University Press, 2014. Shults presses Deleuze into the service of a militant atheism, seeking to extract resources from Deleuze for the construction

---

7. Justaert, *Theology after Deleuze*, 9.

8. John Milbank, *Theology and Social Theory* (Oxford: Blackwell, 2008), 306.

of an iconoclastic theology that can liberate thinking from the oppressive power of images of transcendence. This approach builds on Deleuze's own view, expressed in his book on the painter Francis Bacon, that there is "always an atheism to be extracted from religion" (*WIP*, 92), and that Christianity more than any other religion "contains a germ of tranquil atheism" (*FBLS*, 124).

Simpson, Christopher Ben. *Deleuze and Theology*. London: Bloomsbury, 2012. A helpful survey of the various ways in which Deleuze's thought has been brought into conversation with theological themes. Useful reading for those new to the subject.

Smith, Daniel W., and Henry Somers-Hall, eds. *The Cambridge Companion to Deleuze*. Cambridge: Cambridge University Press, 2012.

Williams, James. *Gilles Deleuze's* Difference and Repetition: *A Critical Introduction and Guide*. Edinburgh: Edinburgh University Press, 2003.

Žižek, Slavoj. *The Fragile Absolute: Or Why the Christian Legacy Is Worth Fighting For*. London: Verso, 2001.

INDEX OF SCRIPTURE

INDEX OF SUBJECTS
AND NAMES

Christopher Watkin (MPhil, PhD, Jesus College, Cambridge) researches and writes on modern and contemporary French thought, atheism, and religion. He works as senior lecturer in French studies at Monash University in Melbourne, Australia, where he lives with his wife, Alison, and son, Benjamin. His recent books include *Thinking through Creation: Genesis 1 & 2 as Tools of Cultural Critique* (2017), *French Philosophy Today: New Figures of the Human in Badiou, Meillassoux, Malabou, Serres and Latour* (2016), *Difficult Atheism: Post-Theological Thinking in Badiou, Meillassoux and Nancy* (2011), and *From Plato to Postmodernism: The Story of Western Culture through Philosophy, Literature and Art* (2011). He is also the author of *Jacques Derrida* (2017), *Michel Foucault* (2018), and *Gilles Deleuze* (2020) in the P&R Great Thinkers series.

He blogs on French philosophy and the academic life at christopherwatkin.com and is a cofounder of audialteram partem.com, a site with the twin aims of bringing evangelical and Reformed theology into deep conversation with modern French philosophy and of encouraging scholars and scholarship working at the nexus of those traditions. You can find him on Twitter @DrChrisWatkin.

ALSO BY CHRISTOPHER WATKIN
FOR THE GREAT THINKER SERIES

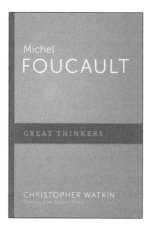

"If you're not familiar with Michel Foucault, you should be. He is one of the most influential figures, if not the most influential figure, in contemporary Western culture. In this volume, Chris Watkin has accomplished what very few have even attempted. He walks us through the development of Foucault's points of view with expert care and clarity. He also compares and contrasts these outlooks with the teachings of the New Testament in ways that challenge followers of Christ to look afresh at some of their most basic commitments. . . . If you haven't read it, you should—today."

    —**Richard L. Pratt Jr.**, President, Third Millennium Ministries

"Chris Watkin has done what I thought was impossible. He has explained Derrida's deconstruction with lucidity, brevity, and charity. Not only that: he has imagined what it would be like for Cornelius Van Til to go toe-to-toe with Derrida in a discussion about language, logic, and the Logos made flesh. . . . Readers who want to know what all the fuss over postmodernity is about would do well to consult this book."

    —**Kevin J. Vanhoozer**, Research Professor of Systematic
      Theology, Trinity Evangelical Divinity School

Did you find this book helpful?
Consider leaving a review online.
The author appreciates your feedback!

Or write to P&R at editorial@prpbooks.com
with your comments. We'd love to hear from you.